AFRICA PRESENTS

THE CONGO RDC

AND

CHILD EDUCATION

FIRST EDITION

BY

BEPONA COLLECTION

Africa presents The Congo RDC

And

Child Education

By

BEPONA COLLECTION

Copyright © 2011 by *BEPONA COLLECTION*

ISBN: 978-0-9859230-4-4

All rights reserved. No part of this book can be reproduced or transmitted in any form by any means, electronic or mechanical, including photocopying, recording, or by any information storage and retrieval system, without the prior written permission of the publisher.

Printed in the Unites States of America

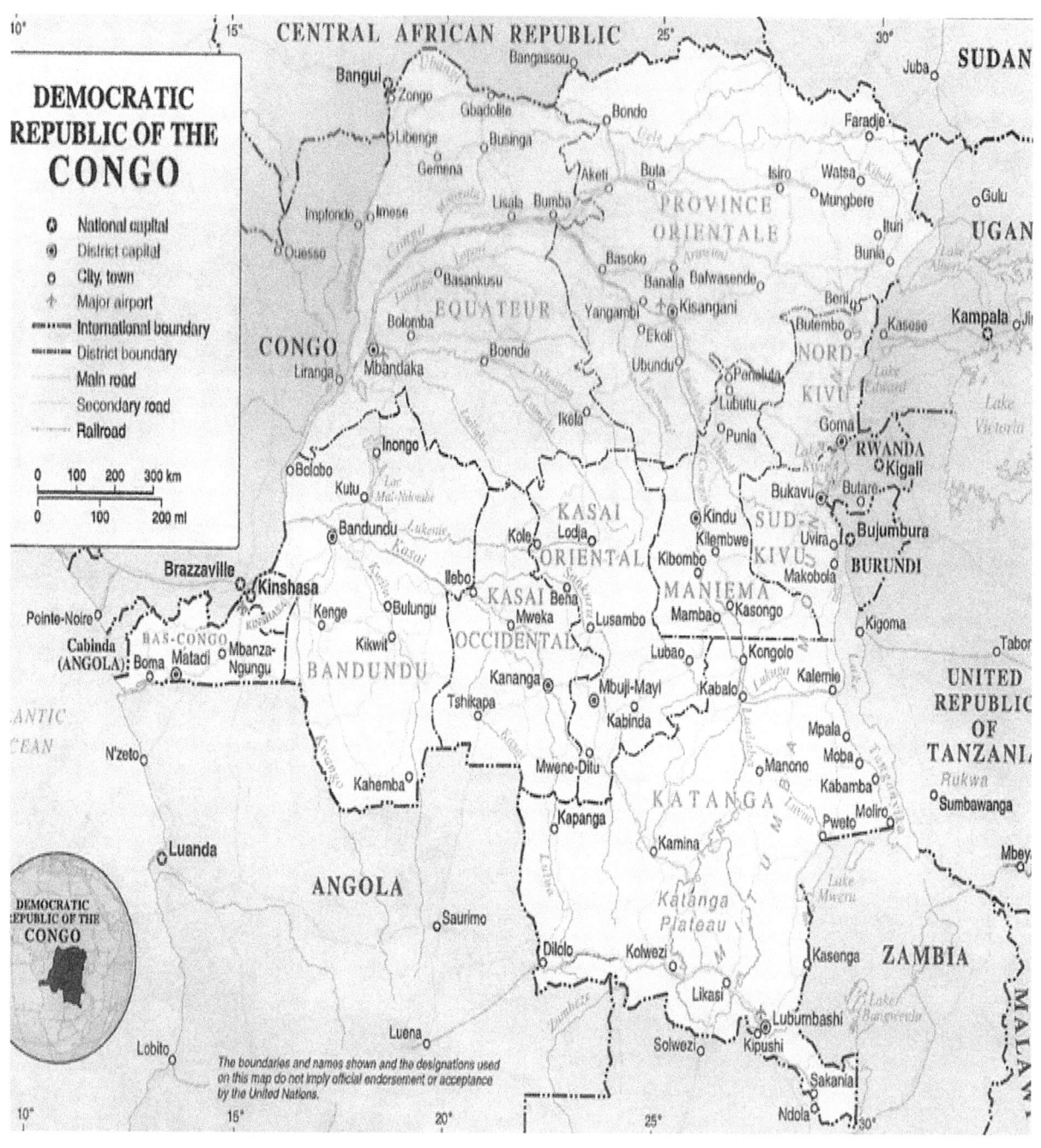

KINSHASA, THE CAPITAL CITY OF THE CONGO, RDC PRIOR TO THE CIVIL WAR

TABLE OF CONTENTS

Page

Dedication………………………………………………………………………..............8

Overview………………………………………………………………………..……….9

INTRODUCTION……………………………………………………………………....23

CHAPTER 1

    Daily Routine…………………………………………………………………..29

    Child's Responsibilities………………………………………………………....31

    Urban Children………………………………………………………………....34

    Developing Child Safety Measures……………………………………..............35

    Congolese Father's View……………………………………………….……….36

    Child Care from Infant to Adulthood…………………………………………...37

CHAPTER 2

    Rules and Regulations………………………………………………………......38

    Addressing People………………………………………………………………41

    Clarifying & Simplifying Terms ……………………………..………………...43

    Clarifying Incest Issues………………………………………….……………...46

    Highlighting appropriate Manners……………………………………………...49

    Children behaviors at Home & In the Society…………………..……………...51

    Child Safety………………………………………………………….………...53

CHAPTER 3

Contrasting Urban vs Rural Areas Students 56

Relationship between Congolese Parents and Their Children...................….....62

CHAPTER 4

Learning Process..66

Cultural Education..72

Rewarding Children for Their Endeavors...90

Celebrating School Achievement..94

Conclusion..95

Word of Appreciation to our Readers...108

Acknowledgement..109

Bepona Collection Books..110

About Bepona Collection...111

Index...117

Dedication

This book is dedicated to all our loved ones (Parents and grandparents) who had nurtured us efficiently from childhood to adulthood. They had revealed relevant information and gave us the insight to look forward in exploring, discovering and restoring our hidden heritage. Further, they had taught us how we should go about developing all the necessary qualities required by the Bantu/Congolese culture in order to become self-sufficient in life, as well as to establish a harmonious society which inspires justice, peace, love and respect to everyone involved. Above all, we are grateful to our Nzambe (uhm-Zambah) God or Nzambi-Mpungu (uhm-Zambah – Uhm-Pungu (The Great Being) who had illumined our ancestors, by endowing them the wisdom and the strength to preserve and sustain the essential facts pertaining to our culture, which had unfortunately been stigmatized for centuries.

Ultimately, our loved ones had disclosed the vital knowledge which the younger generation currently needs in order to discover their hidden African values, as well as to restore their cultural identity. And therefore, we are compelled to share this clear perception, or understanding which we have acquired with all the African Diasporas throughout the world. Finally, we wish to make it available to any individual who is interested in embracing diversity.

Overview of Child Education in Africa Particularly in the Congo RDC

In the Congo RDC, the method of dealing with child education does not require any sophisticated or complicated steps. It does not entail any social science terminologies either. The Congolese style is moderately simple. Parents are naturally gifted, and perpetuate their ancestors' routine of nurturing a child from infancy to maturity.

Certainly, African people believe that the Creator had endowed all the necessary knowledge to their ancestors ever since they were created. Apparently, either prior to the decline of the African civilization, or thereafter, people had been following almost similar routine of rearing children, in the Congo RDC, which is the Bantu society.

Evidently, African parents follow their keen senses when dealing with a child development in its every aspect. Intuitively, they focus on every step of the way, emotional, intellectual, physical, spiritual, and social. In fact, as a child is developing, its parents begin to become more and more alert to those changes. Therefore, they would act accordingly. Practically, parents are so familiar with the traditional procedure of nurturing a child, from its early years to preschool stage and henceforth. It is at the early period that parents begin formulating their observations on emotional and social development of the kid. Usually, that first phase occurs between the ages of two to five years old.

Because parents instinctively, recognize the needs of all their children, they pay special attention to a child who is approaching five to six years old. Naturally, around this time, parents emphasize the child's intellectual need. And therefore, they would put him or her in school in order to begin learning the most important subjects such as Reading, Math and Writing, in a local or a Mission school.

Generally, parents systematically respond to different stages of the development of their child or children, as we have previously indicated. In fact, emotional and social development are observed in the following manners: At the early stage, by observations, parents would convince themselves that their child is expressing the desire of playing with the children of its own age, for instance. And therefore, they would allow, or encourage that child to mingle with the neighbors' kids of its own age, in order to spend time playing together. This fact actually, identifies a child's social needs.

In addition, parents realize that children develop some sort of attraction with each other. This situation can be seen for instance, in the case where a parent is attempting to suddenly pull a child away from its closest friends. Initiating such action could sometimes result to many unpleasant situations. In fact, that child may exhibit some negative reactions due to its parent's swiftly action. While the children are in the course of enjoying each other's company, a child would either begin weeping in order to express its frustration for having interrupted the moment of its fun. Sometimes however, that child would make displeased expression by frowning, and that is to demonstrate its unwillingness to break off from such a pleasant association. Such a reaction can be viewed as a child's intense desire for its social development.

At times, however, parents may notice that attempting to take that child away, vigorously from the atmosphere where he or she is being rejoiced, the child may exemplify different types of peculiar behaviors. A parent or the guardian of that kid may observe that while taking the child to an opposite site, the infant could be struggling to look back towards his or her friends sorrowfully. And every now and then, the child would be pointing its little finger out towards his or her friends whom he or she is leaving behind with a feeling of regret. Furthermore, from time to time, the kid may display another sign by waving at its friends unhappily. Apparently, that type of experience could indicate a proof that that kid is expressing its yearning desire for its social development. And therefore, its playing activities with its friends would need to be satisfied; otherwise, it could generate a negative reaction to that infant.

The above mentioned example can be viewed both as a child's emotional development, as well as his or her social development. The explanation of emotional development can be perceived by that sudden interruption of a child's playtime, which has caused him or her to weep.

The action of weeping demonstrates the fact that the child has been actually hurt emotionally for having broken its temporary relationship with his or her playmates. In other words, the child's feelings have been disturbed, and the joy has been abruptly stopped. It has therefore, been replaced by the feeling of irritation or resentment; apparently, that child was not ready to stop her or his fun at that particular moment. This unexpected situation has actually caused a shock to the kid's feelings. Consequently, the child has become furious. By observations, the Congolese parents would use the following expression, "**Mwan'atomboki**" (Mouan ahtom-bokee), meaning that the child is really annoyed. And therefore, parents must become aware of handling this situation cautiously, by talking to the infant softly, caressing or embracing it lovingly in order to soothe and dissipate its emotional pain.

Obviously, to the African parents, particularly to the Congolese parents, this acknowledgment is intrinsic or innate, so to speak. It does not require the study of "Child Psychology." Naturally, African parents are known as ideal psychologists, as far as nurturing their children is concerned. In fact, since the decline of the African civilization, no written manuscript had been left behind which could possibly be regarded as a source of reference in this area. And therefore, all the facts concerning education had been certainly concealed.

The colonial system on the other hand, had worsened the educational vision; as a result, the ancestors had to hold on into their innate knowledge which was given to them by "Nzambe-Mpungu (uhm-Zahmbay-uhm-Pungu, their Creator, God." This is the reason why the oral traditions remain exclusively reliable authentic instrument, or the only educational sourcing which African people now possess. Additionally, concerning emotional and social development, parents may observe sometimes the joy, which excels from their child when he or she, suddenly, encounters his or her little friends. The child gets all excited, or pulls itself away from a parent's arms; and then, drops itself quickly down on the floor. Shortly afterward, the infant begins darting with such an excitement towards its friend or a group of its friends in order to joyously mingle with each other.

Apparently, children forget about their parents at that particular moment of ecstasy, because they are under a joyful and harmonious atmosphere with their little friends. This is another example, which shows the evidence of social development which the parents are required to understand; and also, be cooperative with the child's needs, which means, allowing the kid to socialize with its own kind. We do not however, allude that children's associations are always harmonious, because they do fight sometimes among themselves. Nevertheless, the beauty of kids' association is the fact that they are not resentful.

Concerning physical development, the parents keep on viewing the child development's process as time goes by, until it reaches its preschool age. A that point, parents allow the child to begin exerting its little energy through her or his tiny muscles. They actually assist in this process by allowing a child to perform simple physical tasks, such as carrying a plate from one area to another around the house, or placing a cup on the table; or sometimes, bringing a piece of fruit to his daddy, mother or to its siblings. That child's actions can therefore, be termed as its physical development as it has been previously stated. In fact, the physical task increases gradually and proportionately with the child's age. This fact can also be viewed as being a natural process to the Congolese parents.

In effect, for religious families, this is also the time which the child is gradually exposed to his or her spiritual development. The child is taught how to begin saying its prayers, addressed to NZAMBE (**uhm-Zahmbah**) or Nzambi-Mpungu (**uhm-Zambe-uhm-Pungu -** The Great Being). Additionally, parents begin, gradually raising the child's awareness of the Lord Jesus Christ and His divine attributes. This is when the Christian children start eagerly developing their devotion and adoration to Jesus Christ and the practice of the monotheism, as opposed to the children that come from the pagan families who persist to find justifications in the practice of their beliefs in the little gods as well as their practice of all sort of charms, fetishes and all ungodly rituals associated with such belief; and so often referring to the spiritual abuse of the early catholic missionaries. Nonetheless, deep down those individuals had heard the existence of a *Great Being* whom the Congolese ancestors termed, based on the region and the language spoken, ***as*** *either,"* NKOLO *(uhn-Kolo)* – NZAMBE *(uhm-Zahmbay)* in *Lingala language, Nzambi-Mpungu in Kikongo language, and Mungu in Swahili. Nevertheless all these titles were referred to the acknowledgement of a Great Being, residing way in heaven whose power is invincible, as opposed to that of all the little gods down here. Ultimately, this spiritual secret had been already embedded deep down in the hearts of the African ancestors, and it was present prior to the arrival of the early Catholic missionaries in the "Kingdom of Kongo." Obviously, it would be imperative for every African child to be made aware of its ancestors' Traditional or common law, and talk about it with reverence, also learn to conserve and defend it thoroughly*

(**Read "Africa presents the Congo RDC and Traditional Law.**)

Furthermore, a child is taught the appropriate manners of addressing immediate and extended family members (example: "Mama or mah (mother), Papa (father), big sister or big brother (Yaya-*yah-yah*); further, grandmother or grandfather are both called (**Koko** in Lingala language and **Nkaka (uhn-kah-kah** in Kikongo language).

Moreover, children learn the appropriate means of addressing people outside of their family cycle, such as friends or acquaintances. In fact, out of respect, those individuals should be addressed, by prefacing their first names with an appropriate title (example, Mama Bitabe (Mrs. Bitabe), Papa Bitabe (Mr. Bitabe).

Further, in this book, we will explain the connotation of the titles "Mama" and "Papa" as they appear in this context.

Whenever a child is asked for instance, to call an individual who could be standing nearby, or in an adjacent room, the child is already aware that it must preface that particular individual's name with an appropriate title related to that person's gender.

According to the Bantu/Congolese culture, it would appear derogatory to that particular individual, if that child would omit prefacing his or her name with an appropriate title. Those parents, in that case, are held accountable in the society in regard to that kid's behavior. This could actually be regarded as an intellectual development for a child, because it is learning the crucial information required to make a distinction between offensive terms as well as the acceptable or polite terms.

It is imperative for the children to be made aware of this nuance while they are still young. This practice comes naturally to the Congolese children, because parents initiate them since their early days. They have been instructed that utilizing belittling words is morally and culturally unacceptable in our society.

As a result, children are held accountable for their behaviors, because they are supposed to recall all the instructions received from their families at their early years, perpetually.

Physiological Maturity

Generally, as children are reaching the stage of physiological maturity, at this point, both parents begin to become more and more vigilant in regard to those changes, to live harmoniously with their associations in life. Parents highlight the topics such as preventing them from becoming **egocentric** individuals in the society. Also they would stress the reason why children should avoid practicing any types of exploitations of their fellow beings. In this respect, parents would sound a warning of the law of restitution, or a payback time. This natural law is also known as the law of cause and effect, which is inevitable in life. In African culture it is referred to as a *"Curse."*

Additionally, children are taught the practice of **SHARING** with their siblings, their family members, as well as with their friends who are in needs. Good parents also, warn their children from practicing the spirit of **SELFISHNESS**, as that would cause anger and resentment around the family, as well as in the society overall.

And above all, parents insist on the fact that kids should be instructed how to be compassionate and courteous in their association. So, in regard to their physical appearance, kids are referred to their ancestors' refinement.

Ancestors wore high quality fabric, designed with taste. And therefore, children should stick to that ancestral image, which is a part of their heritage.

Moreover, a female parent emphasizes on the topics which a girl needs to learn cautiously, and become aware of it forever, and that is, *the cleansing of her body, especially, its private parts is regarded to be crucial.* In addition, the household duties are also necessary for a girl to learn, as far as her mother is concerned. This particular task needs to be mastered. It is regarded as a fundamental area which a future mother of the society has to know thoroughly in regard to managing her household affairs.

A male parent, on the other hand, ought to lay emphasis on the areas which his son should gradually develop, throughout his entire life. The boy should be taught also how and why he should focus on his male's stamina. The father would explain to his boy or a future father of a society, everything that he would need to acquire his maturity such as all the necessary tools required in life which may help him to master all his manhood responsibilities. Further, due to that ability, he would become a good man, an ideal husband, as well as a perfect father, capable in maintaining a family.

Thus, those attributes would qualify him to make a positive contribution in the Bantu society. Additionally, a good father would never omit mentioning the following statement to his son: "Son, remember that good women, in the Congolese society, are very selective with respect to marriage. Women prefer men who are ambitious. Today, you appear as a boy, but in the future, you will become a man. And therefore, you will need to get married. Thus, in order to be accepted by a good woman, you need to have an aspiration and resilience in life. Also, you ought to bear in mind that maintaining a refined outlook aspect is required. And failure to honor these instructions, and if you choose to neglect developing your African man's stamina, while you are still young; then son, you will have a cause to regret it. So, just keep in mind that people are prone to criticize you and condemn your folks for having failed to shape you properly, and lay emphasis on your cultural education, that is, if you choose to become a lethargic individual in the society. So, be courageous in facing the various challenges of this world."

In essence, Congolese parents stress the following statement, "Child, now that we are all alive, make sure to open your eyes and perceive things which are being disclosed to you. Also, be alert, and listen carefully to every instruction that you are currently receiving from your folks. Above all, you need to ask questions, and learn from the source from where you would receive genuine historical facts which you will have to impeccably transmit likewise, to your future children. Remember this well, because you would never get any authentic knowledge outside of your own family; and certainly, there would be no written book which might reveal all the details regarding your traditions or your ancestors' heritage, except the concealment of your real knowledge.

So, what then would your children learn? They would unfortunately learn fragmentary historical fact full of imperfection. And therefore, do not neglect the instructions which you are now receiving." With this respect, the French people said, *"On est mieux servi que par soi-même," (Serving oneself is much better than being served.)*

Further, bear in mind that in life, an individual is required to make a crucial decision concerning the things he or she wishes to accomplish in life, as well as the location from where he or she would wish to settle down. Be aware that even our grandparents knew how to make that intelligent choice. They used to move across the land, until they would finally find a suitable area where they would decide to settle down. It would be wise trying to take that approach, for a security reason. The land belongs to our ancestors, we can move around however we wish, as long as we remain conscious of our Nzambe/Nzambi-Mpungu/Mungu, our God, and also respect our ancestors' virtues.

The areas to settle down would vary from urban, rural, or even in those small towns. In fact, in order to make such a decision, you would need to first inquire, and then, make a contrast between advantages and disadvantages of living in those areas. In actual fact, it would be necessary to become acquainted with the fact that living in the urban area, for instance, nowadays would entail that the individual would have to purchase every single commodity in order to make a living. There is no alternative in this area! Whereas, if you opt to reside in the rural areas, you would have to face various alternatives of making a living; through physical work naturally such as tilling, fixing ponds, fishing, and conducting some trading activities either from your farms, or from the villages to various small towns where you would be obligated to interact with foreign merchants whose motives are basically destructive." So, beware, for most of them are undercover kidnappers of our robust uncles, aunts as well as cousins.

In fact, our folks have sounded a warning to that effect. So, beware! Those individuals act cunningly. They disguise themselves as innocents store owners during the days, or as good merchants. And yet, when the nights come, their true evil activities begin; running their big trucks along the dark roads. And then, stopping at every occasion to apprehend our innocents loved ones, walking down the roads, in the attempt to returning back to their respective homes. And therefore, beware, should you happen to interact with all those foreign merchants in the future, just remain alert at all times. You should just try not to fall into such ensnare."

Ultimately, good African parents are known to be very protective of their children. They feel that children should be made aware of the past and present historical events, so that they may be prepared to face all the current challenges involved in our contemporary era.

It is preferable to teach the kids, all the necessary historical facts concerning their culture without any reservation, and also stressing on the fact that they need to endeavor in becoming self-sufficient, and gain respect in the society. Furthermore, children should be taught how to become strong enough in restoring, maintaining and sustaining their cultural values, which have been unfortunately stigmatized for several decades. Additionally, it would be necessary to make children aware that developing a high degree of apprehensiveness against the usurpers would be highly recommended; as such concept would help them to protect themselves, their resources as well as their cultural identity.

Concerning school education in the Congo RDC, due to the incessant wars in the country, the educational system has been completed devastated since the year 2001 up to these days. Although, many children are still eager to attend school, and they are willing to learn so that they too could acquire the knowledge from our modern technology, however, they are being hindered by several economical, as well as political obstacles; consequently, this impasse is generating a large amount of destitute families and orphans. This dilemma certainly is causing a high level of illiterate in this land.

INTRODUCTION

Child Education in the Congo RDC

This is an example of the Congolese Children

Zuka Kayalu (boy) and Asala Kayalu (girl)

We will see, throughout this book, how the Congolese parents and their children interact with each other in terms of education. We have actually developed the course of "Child Education," based on our own personal research, observations as well as our own oral traditions. In the Bantu/Congolese culture, the course of "Child Education" is designed in such a natural way. It does not require any predetermined concepts or pre-established rules.

This picture depicts two children: Zuka Kayalu (boy), 4 years old and Asala Kayalu (girl), 2 years old. Both of these children will help us to perceive how they are being raised and educated by their parents, Mr. Ezombo and Mrs. Mangeli Kayalu.

In reality, Congolese parents view themselves as the hearts of preschool education to their children. In most cases, parents begin childhood education around the house from the age of two to five years old; and then, gradually parents continue to put an emphasis on the most important elements which children should actually become aware of, around the family, as well as in the society, in general. Apparently, the basic education may vary slightly from family to family. It is also based on different geographical areas. Further, it depends on the environment from where the child is being reared. Based on the child's behaviors, however, it is sometimes possible to conclude whether the child has been raised in the rural, the urban or in small town areas. Further, it is easy to detect whether or not that child comes from a high or a modest class family, based on that child's demeanor.

Basically, parents feel that the early childhood learning is crucial to a child, because that is the appropriate time to start shaping the kid's behaviors emotionally, mentally, physically, spiritually, and socially. It seems as though the parents are actually planting a seed in the child's brain, which will in effect blossom in the future, and will eventually help to determine the kid's prospect behaviors with respect to its ability to cope with life. Furthermore, parents judge that the betterment and refinement of a child begin with the home education. That is the right time to lay emphasis on social and cultural norms as well as on religious beliefs within a child's brain.

According to the Congolese parents, the preliminary step in child education is the mouth hygiene. The parents stress on the cleaning of a child's body and its teeth on the daily basis. The goal is to keep the teeth immaculately clean without any black spot, or any yellowish color appearance. Parents feel that this actually is a targeted area, and therefore, it should be accentuated in a child's mind without fail. Further, it should be reminded repeatedly.

Example of a Congolese Family (Ex -Kayalu)

Mr. Ezombo Kayalu (father) - Mrs. Mangeli Lituka (mother)

Zuka (boy) and Asala (girl).

The Congolese culture requires that parents ought to remain in a very close association with their children. In fact, it is not African norms for parents to abandon their infants or children due to a financial dilemma, or any others. Taking such an approach would appear as committing a crime to the Congolese society. Due to their parents' love, Congolese children feel obligated to remain so attached to their parents, as well. They actually care for their folks, and are eager to satisfy their basic needs without fail, so long as they remain on this earth. The Congolese children demonstrate a lot of respect to their parents. It does not matter whether they are literate or illiterate; respect remains the key word, because the word GRATITUDE will continue to ring that bell in their ears.

LEARNING EXPERIENCE

Infant First Lesson

The mother takes the initiative of teaching her son, **Kiesi (Keyase) Muwela (Muwala)** his first lesson. That lesson is a seating position. Although, the infant appears fearful in this unusual position, his mother's hand is supporting him from his back; and it is reassuring Kiesi's safety. The infant's mother is inviting him to let go without fear. What the mother is actually saying is, "My child, trust fully in your mother's strength and wisdom, because she had vowed to care for you, and that until the day you will reach the age of maturity." Certainly, you shall follow after my footsteps in terms of caring for your own offspring with a genuine love when you shall become a father or a foundation of our future society."

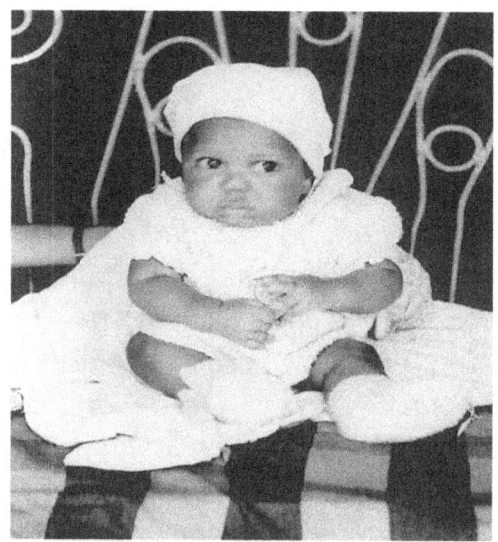

This is Kiesi Muwela

This picture will always remind Kiesi of the loving care which he had received from his beloved mother while he was still an infant. Kiesi will honor the old saying, "Hands ought to be crossed," this simply means that when you have received, remember to give back in the future, the bottom line is that "Do not be Selfish in life!"

27
A Child's Vision Creates His Future

Djemba Munkalu is an orphan. He is 4 years old.
Djemba is being raised by his maternal aunt who is struggling to nurture him. *Please notice this child's faith and his confidence.* His aunt had already taught him all the relevant elements which her nephew needs to comprehend at this age according to the Bantu/Congolese culture.

Djemba Munkalu has already a vision at this age. Therefore, he loves going to school. He listens to his aunt's advice attentively. He had learned how to clean his teeth and his body well upon awakening in the morning. Munkalu knows how to say his daily prayers. He knows who "Nzambe or Nzambi-Mpungu (the Great Being)" is, as well as the Lord Jesus Christ. He also remembers to wash his hands prior to eating his meals and thereafter. In addition, he does his homework diligently.

Djemba Munkalu has a dream. His firm desire is to become a teacher one day in his life. The child does not think about any obstacle that might hinder him from achieving his set goal. The child's faith actually begins at his early age. He is trusting that his aunt would continue to support him, although in reality she is struggling to finance his education as well as rearing him. Nevertheless, this child continues to confirm, "I will become a teacher when I grow up, because my aunt loves me and she takes care of me."

Child's Ability and Confidence

Meet Luzolo Zundi three years old

Luzolo Zundi came from a happy family. He loves to sing gospel music. Luzolo's hobby is to watch a soccer game along with his father. He gets really into it, and follows the soccer players' movement as he watches them play on TV. The boy jerks and participates in his mind with his favorite players' steps. Lozolo is such a bright and courageous boy. He has sharp eyes and good perception. Lozolo is an outspoken child.

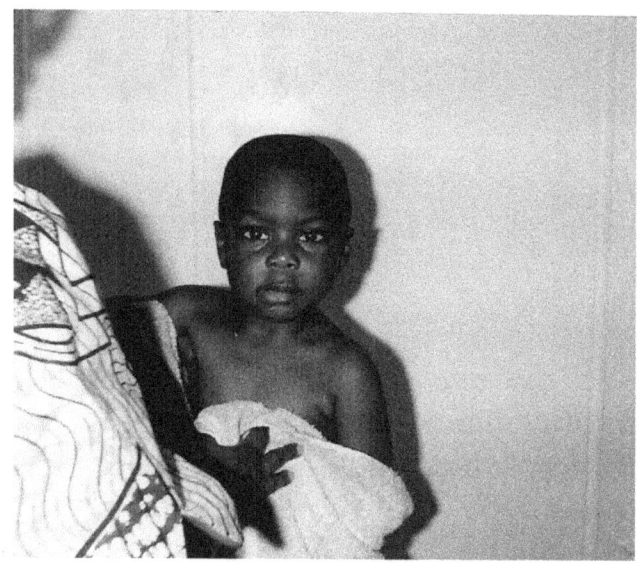

Luzolo is a remarkable child. He exhibits sens of responsibility and confidence at his very younger age. At the age of 3, he claims his independence from his parents. He tells his parents at their every attempt to assist him in terms of his personally hygiene that,"Oh, no!" Luzolo would exclaim! "No, Mom, watch, let me show you that I know how to bath and brush my own teeth by myself." Her mother would be standing nearby watching Luzolo doing everything nicely and quickly! Even after taking his bath, Lozolo would select his own towel and keep himself dried.

Luzolo is a bright and a loving little boy. He tells his parents every morning, "I love you." Lozolo is so observant, and he notices everything that his mother does for him each day! He then, tells his mother, caressing her hands, "Mah, you love me and I love .too. Mah, I will buy you a car when I grow up." He watches sports along with his father. Lozolo's dream is to become a professional Soccer player.

CHAPTER 1

Daily Routine

Usually, Congolese parents begin teaching their children all the basic daily routines, systemically, according to their culture. Through this book, we shall illustrate practically all the necessary steps involved in this subject.

Parents begin highlighting hygiene teaching from the age of three years old and up. Children are taught that nothing should be put in their mouths as soon as they awaken in the morning. The prior step upon awakening in the morning is the washing of their bodies and the cleaning of their teeth. The mouth should be kept immaculately clean and fresh prior to thinking about eating any type of food. It is a standard pattern of behavior to begin by cleaning their teeth with a special wooden stick (called **Nzete (uhn-zahtay - ya Mino (meeno) in Lingala language** or "**Nti (uhn-tee ya Meno (maynou)**" in **Kikongo language**) designed to clean teeth thoroughly. (*Read Africa presents the Congo RDC and Lingala or Kikongo language.*)

- The plants that are used in the cleaning of teeth grow in a natural state, or they are uncultivated, so to speak. Further, they are not toxic, and our ancestors have used them for centuries. And therefore, the wooden sticks originated from those trees are highly recommended to be used by adults, as well as children without fear of damaging their teeth, or even causing any adverse effects internally or externally.

- Each child should be made aware of having his or her own personal small wooden stick called "Nzete (uhn-Zah-tah) ya Mino (meenou)" until it diminishes gradually, based on the daily usage. The parents should therefore remain alert in noticing whether or not the child's wooden stick needs to be replaced with a new one, in a timely manner. It is not wise to let the child walk around without cleaning its teeth for the entire day. In the cities however, individuals have options. They can choose between using tooth paste and tooth brush from utilizing wooden stick (nzete ya mino), if they so desire. However, they prefer natural usage of a wooden stick, because it keeps their teeth very clean, white and fresh.

CHILD'S RESPONSIBILITIES

In order to prevent criticism, the children are made aware of their mouths hygiene; otherwise people would scoff at that child, and especially at his parents. Neighbors and others would actually start murmuring and pointing out fingers at that kid, saying, "Look at that child, he or she had rotten and yellowish teeth, which resemble to a **Squirrel's teeth**!"

People may also add the following remark, "His or her parents do not teach him or her how to keep his or her teeth clean." The outsiders would therefore conclude that, "If a child had rotten and yellowish appearance teeth that would naturally imply that the child's parents have neglected to teach it the appropriate mouth hygiene." Eventually, parents are always to blame, because the child is only a victim of circumstance.

Children certainly, should be trained systematically from the beginning, so that they would be accustomed with such routine. They would afterward endeavor to keep their teeth always immaculate. And noticing this fact, their teachers or people around the children would eventually respect their parents. However, parents would be criticized strongly when the children do not meet that high standard. So, *the Mouth Hygiene is Crucial in the Congolese Culture!*

Children are also instructed to wash hands thoroughly prior to handling of anything to eat, and thereafter. Further, parents educate their children to also learn how to cover their mouths, when coughing and sneezing, in order to prevent germs coming in or going out. In addition, children are warned not to drink from the same glass or cup which has been used by somebody else. This instruction does not exclude family members or close friends. It actually has one purpose that is to prevent the spreading of germs. Further, kids have been advised, never to take a sip or a bite from another person's drink or food. If there is a need to share, it would be preferable to cut a piece of that substance either manually, or with a knife. Liquid substance is to be shared pouring it into another container.

In essence, religious families instruct their children to always, begin saying a short prayer of gratitude to God prior to eating their meals. They also should be thankful to their parents who had brought forth the money to provide the food for the family. Further, after the blessing of their food, children should also bless the cook (usually Mama) who had lovingly taken the initiative of putting the dishes together.

Additionally, parents stress on the fact that kids should learn how to be thankful for anything that is being offered them, regardless to its nature. Moreover, religious parents are required to make it mandatory for their children to form the habit of being appreciative rather than taking things for granted. With this respect, some parents had formed the habit of confiscating momentarily, the item that was offered to the child who did not remember to always say, "Thank you," until it does.

In fact, many Congolese parents had actually demonstrated this instruction to the children who had forgotten to say "Thank you," or those who had shown disobedience from following the parents' rule. Children who are asked to state the reason why the item had been taken away from their hands, *a smart child would spontaneously respond, "Oh, I know why! It is because I forgot to say thank you!"* And then, at that time, the child will impulsively remember to say "Thank you, usually with a little smile accompanying her reply; also adding either, Mama, Papa, or to any other adult or even siblings. After this incident, the guardian or parents would give back that particular item to the kid; and, because that child has finally complied with its family's rule. *This is how the well bred Congolese children are to be trained.*

In fact, it is vitally important for any well bred Congolese child to make sure that the above mentioned instructions are practiced daily.

URBAN CHILDREN

THE PICTURES BELOW DEPICT CHILDREN THAT ARE BEING RAISED IN THE URBAN AREAS.

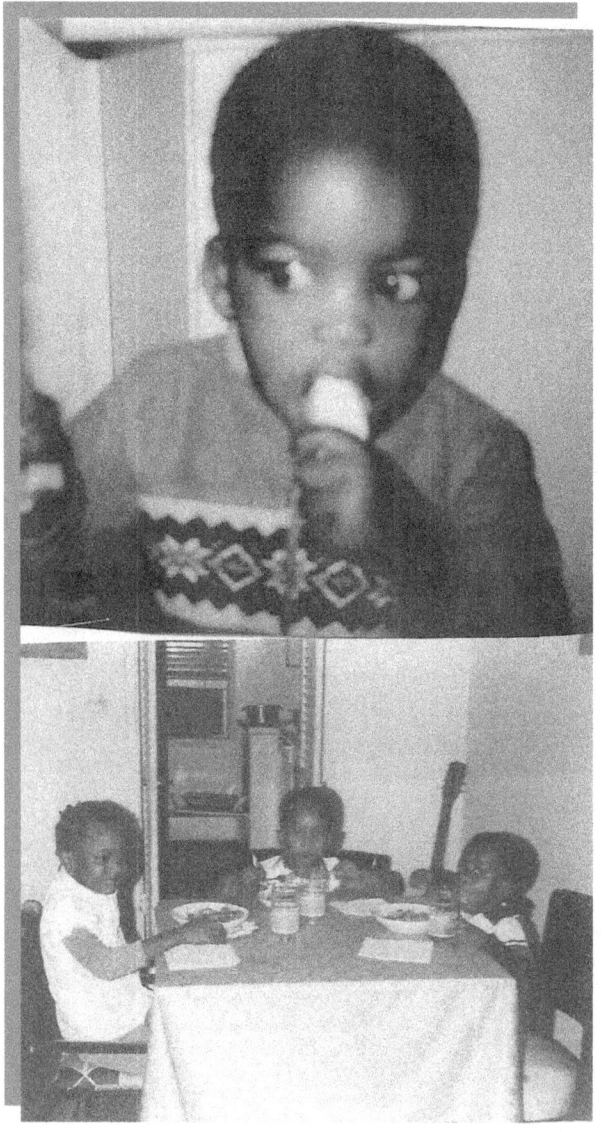

Telama, Sasuka and Matondo, Jr.

Matala Bolingo is 2 year old. He is mastering his self-feeding lesson. **Matala** would never let anyone else feed him, besides from his own parents. Matala would nod his head in the attempt to reject food from unfamiliar person. These are safety measures for this child, as far as his parents are concerned. No individual would ever succeed feeding this child any unwanted substance.

Telema (girl), **Sasuka** and **Matondo** (boys)– Matondo family taught their children how to sit at the dinner table and eat their meals respectfully. Children had been also warned never to eat food given by a stranger. They do respect the instructions which they have received. Because of that, children would always waggle their heads left and right to refuse any unwanted offer.

DEVELOPPING CHILD SAFETY MEASURES AT HOME

Parents instruct their children regarding safety measures. In fact, they stress on the following statement, "Do not accept or eat anything given to you by a stranger, because you do not know the nature and the origin of that thing!" Parents repeatedly overstress, or emphasize this particular topic to their children as a part of child education in the Bantu/Congolese culture.

This education is considered to be vitally important due to diverse abuses which had been reported in the past around the country concerning children protection. Apparently, the migrations of various populations throughout the country, as well as the presence of the foreign traders or merchants, have created all sort of dilemma in the country. In addition, parents highlight another topic which is, "Never to accept any money given to you by a stranger either, because that is, usually known as a "Filthy Money" associated with unpleasant outcomes, according to the Congolese ancestors' beliefs." Furthermore, "A child should not be allowed to go to any friend's house without its parents' authorization. Moreover, it is preferable not to permit a child to form the habit of eating at people's homes." Parents warn their children on the above issues repeatedly. Children who show disobedience would have to undergo a severe punishment.

Due to the incessant dangerous situations within the Land, the Congolese parents teach their children to remain at home, especially when parents are absent. This is the reason why Congolese children are skeptical to any unfamiliar individual who might appear around them, or who may attempt to enter their property, whenever their parents are away from their home.

S A F E T Y

A CONGOLESE FATHER'S VIEW

How a Congolese Father Feels about His Son or Daughter?

Mr. Bandu and his son, Bandu, Jr.

LOVING CARE

A Congolese father feels obligated to share his love with his beloved child, especially a son. Further, he believes that a child needs his parents' affection in order to be healthy and developed happily. The father deems also that a well bred child will build a constructive society, which will be full of joy and respect. Therefore, it is my duty, as a father, to make my child feel my deepest love while he is still young.

When I love my son, he will pass my love to the next generation which will spread the love of God to everyone who shall live in our society, and those throughout the world. My love is a powerful weapon which will help my son to cope with the pressure of this modern world.

Child Care from Infant to Adulthood

This is **Boyita Munduya**, she is one year old

Boyita *is receiving her parents' attention and love, on a daily basis. She is a very happy child. Her parents feel that she will be successful in life, because she is growing in a joyful environment. And therefore, when she grows up, she will eventually have something positive or constructive to share with her community. Her parents realize that it is their obligation to nurture her appropriately.*

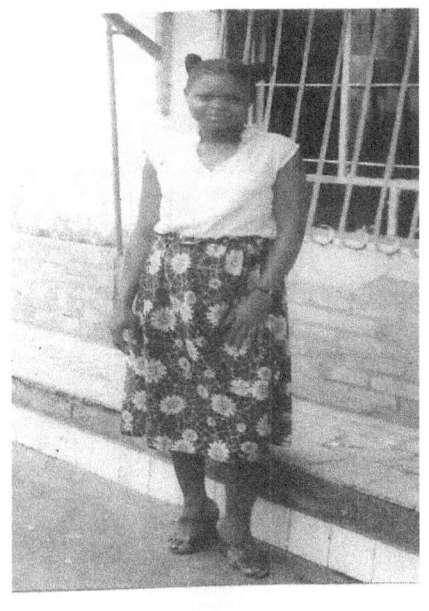

*This is **Boyita**. She has reached 17 years old now. Boyita is now attending high school. Her aspiration is to become a family Doctor, so that she would help everyone, especially her parents, when they will grow old. Boyita is aware that she comes from a modest family. However, she also acknowledges the fact that her parents are determined to secure her future. She is therefore, determined not to abuse her parents' trust in her.*

CHAPTER 2

RULES AND REGULATIONS

What is not authorized around the house according to Kayalu family? Their children should be aware of the following rules:

- No screaming or fighting with each other – No violence is allowed around the family.

- Should any discrepancy arise between children; it ought to be reported to the parents who have the ability of settling it harmoniously.

- No retaliation is permitted among the children. Disobedience would result in a punishment.

- The use of any indecent words around the house, or around the elders is absolutely forbidden, because that demonstrates a sign of impertinence; and therefore it would result to a severe punishment to any child who seems not to be submissive.

- Children are not permitted to drink coffee, wine or liquor, but water. Coffee and wine are considered to be too strong and harmful substance to the children's nervous system, it causes a child to become hyperactive, according to the culture. Finally, the Congolese parents stress on the fact that Children are

- not allowed under any circumstances to take anything that belong to somebody else!" without having any authorization from the owner, because that activity is known as "*STEALING.*

- It is vitally important to remind all the children from their childhood that the act of *"STEALING"* or any types of swindling activities just **STINKS**! Therefore, every child should be warned from the beginning that an individual, who steals from another person, has no value in the eyes of his or her family members, or friends, and especially in the eyes of Nzambe, our Great **God**. *STEALIN*G is actually an awful action which is reserved only to the ***LAZY and ENVIOUS PEOPLE. Those*** *who undervalue themselves, or their families' dignity!*

Therefore, a child is taught from its early days that "When you grow up, you must work in order to earn a living. You should also ensure not to dishonor your God, your family, as well as your community. Therefore, try not to get enmeshed in such activities." You might ask, why not? We shall answer, "Because it will bring a **Curse** in your life, sooner or later, *according to the Congolese ancestors' beliefs."*

How should a child or children act outside of their parents' home, based on Kayalu family's rules? -
(Child's behavior in public)

- Show respect to everyone and especially to the elderly people or those individuals who are in the child's parents' age category.

- Never start any fight with anybody. Therefore, any child who will misbehave will be subject to a punishment, should that incident be directly reported by any eyewitness to the child's parents.

- The type of punishment could be either "kneeling for an hour, or the child could undergo a different kind of punishment depending on the parents' preference or choice.

EDUCATION IN KAYALU (Kah-yah-lou) FAMILY

A Congolese family, ***called Kayalu*** - Mrs. Mangeli Kayalu and Mr. Ezombo Kayalu had two children, a boy and a girl, as it was previously stated. The boy named Zuka Kayalu and a girl was called Asala Kayalu. Basically, it is a well known fact for the children to repeat things which they hear from their parents, on a regular basis. Children also attempt to do things, which their parents do regularly.

Demonstration of children behaviors

Mr. Kayalu and his wife became aware of their children's actions as time went by. As soon as the children reached three and five years old, the couple began noticing peculiar behaviors from both children. Whenever the husband would call his wife by her first name, such as "Mangeli," the children would repeat after their father "Mangeli," instead of calling their mother, **"Mama."** Further, every time that Mrs. Kayalu would call her husband by his first name, **"Ezombo,"** the children would also repeat the name, calling their father, "Ezombo," instead of calling him **Papa.**

ADDRESSING PEOPLE PROPERLY

Generally, from the age of two and on, the Congolese parents begin to gently educate their children, because they believe that it is better to start educating children at their early age rather than waiting until they are much older. Parents actually apply the old saying, "Shape the tree while it is still tiny, in that way, it will not grow out of shape." It is indeed true that, prevention is better than cure, as the old saying goes. Therefore, it would be strenuous attempting to redress a child once he or she has been accustomed with inappropriate manners."

Therefore, a well bred Congolese child is taught the suitable terminologies of addressing their immediate parents, their siblings, as well as their grandparents since early childhood.

Parents are actually known as genealogists to their children. Kids learn family history such as (the name of their tribe, the area of their parents' origin, including the name of the language spoken in their native village, as well their main dish or food which their tribe eat on a regular basis.). Further, they are taught the appropriate manners of addressing friends or acquaintances, young and old people based on their gender.

- ***Mrs. and Mr. Kayalu told the children***: "Remember that children are not allowed to call their parents by name, because that is considered to be a "Taboo" in our Congolese culture. It is contempt to your parents. Children must always address their parents honorably, such as, "Mama or Mah (for a female parent)," and "Papa (for a male parent or Tata)." Remember also that, when calling immediate parents, children should never mention their first names either. You should just say "Mama" or "Papa" until you attract parents' attention. This is how the children must address their immediate parents. **Zuka and Asala – Do you understand now? Both children Answered, *"Yes, Papa, yes Mama."***

In fact, children are actually innocent; and they would indeed follow whatever instructions given them from their childhood. In essence, any subject that is related to the traditional law should always be addressed with reverence; this means, it is being referred to our ancestors' wisdom. And therefore, any subject that is socially or culturally prohibited, in the Bantu/Congolese culture, such thing is also considered to be legally prohibited as far as the Traditional law is concerned. So, when teaching children, parents always state: "Beware acting or doing such and such thing, because that is against our ancestors' law. In Lingala language, it is stated – **Mibeko** (meebako) **Ya** (yah) **Ba** (bay) **KOKO** (koh-koh); - *Please read the book "Africa presents the Congo RDC and Lingala language." In Kikongo language, however, this expression is referred to as, "**NSIKU** (uhn-seekou) **Ya** (yah) **Ba** (bah) **Mbuta** (uhn-bou-tah) – Please read the book, "Africa presents the Congo RDC and Kikongo language.*

In effect, as we have explained so far in this book, the same truth is stated in all the Congolese languages. **And therefore, anything or topic that is forbidden on grounds of being sacred must be spoken with reverence in honor to our ancestors' wisdom.**

Clarifying and Simplifying Terms to Children

One day, Zuka Kayalu, the boy, heard his father calling his mother by her first name," Mangeli!" The boy asked his father,"*How is it that you are calling mama Mangeli then?* **"Aren't you supposed to call her mama too**?" Mr. and Mrs. Kayalu had found this question somewhat hilarious at first, and they both laughed spontaneously about it. Suddenly, however, Mr. Kayalu whispered, and said to his wife, "Mangeli, as funny as it might sound, the child needs a genuine answer." He continued, "Mangeli, notice the look at Zuka's face. He is frowning, this actually is an indication that he desires to have a clear and genuine answer to his seeming complicated question. He apparently wants it, immediately." Zuka's eyes were focused on his father's face. The boy appeared puzzled, because he wanted to hear that genuine answer quickly.

PARENTS REALISED THE ISSUE NEEDED TO BE ADDRESSED

Mr. and Mrs. Kayalu called Asala, the girl, to come and join Zuka, so that she too, could learn from her brother's question. Finally, four of them sat down next to each other, and simultaneously, the parents seized the opportunity to educate them regarding this particular subject and many others such as the practice of **Selfishness, Violence,** or of **Fraudulent transactions** which are all regarded as TABOO in the Bantu/Congolese culture, meaning that all of them are against our ancestors' beliefs."

READERS SHOULD BEAR IN MIND THAT SINCE THERE ARE NO PRE-DEFINED STEPS FOR CHILD EDUCATION SUBJECT IN THE BANTU/CONGOLESE CULTURE, PARENTS EDUCATE THEIR CHILDREN BASED ON OBSERVATIONS OF THEIR DAILY ACTIONS AND BEHAVIORS – PARENTS WOULD SEIZE THAT OPPORTUNITY AND WOULD EXPLAIN THAT TOPIC CLEARLY, AND TRYING TO ELABORATE IT AS MUCH AS THEY CAN AND BREAK IT DOWN TO THE LEVEL WHERE THE KIDS CAN GRASP IT A THAT TIME. PARENTS WILL CONTINUE TO ADDRESS THESE TOPICS AS TIME GOES ON.

Basically Mr. Kayalu began by giving his son Zuka a credit for having raised such an intelligent question, ***"Why don't I call Mangeli, "Mama" as you do, he asked Zuka?*** The reason is this Zuka, Mr. Kayalu replied, "Because **Mangeli is not my mother, but she is my wife. I am rather her husband, and I am not her father."**

Then, he continued, "Zuka, one day you will grow up, and become a big man like your papa. And then, you will get married to a woman. That lady whom you will have to marry shall be known as your wife. Further, that woman shall actually call you my husband. The children whom you and your wife will have, they will have to call your wife "**Mama,**" because she is the mother of your child or your children. Furthermore, they will have to call you "**Papa," because you are their father.** Therefore, you should know that a husband is allowed to call his wife by her first name, like I have been calling your mama, **Mangeli**. You cannot call your wife Mama, **OK. Zuka**?" Mr. Kayalu told his son. The boy, Zuka replied, ***"Yes, Papa****."*

Then Zuka asked another question, "but *if Asala (sister) and I get married, can I then, call **Asala**, my wife*?" Both parents busted laughing spontaneously, and then, replied, "Oh! No! Zuka! Such thing is a **Taboo.** It can never be done in our Bantu/Congolese society, practically not in many others, either." Zuka, the bold little boy, continued his inquiry. He said, *"Why can't I do that, Papa?"*

According to our ancestors' sacred wisdom, "children are given the following advice: "Open your eyes and try to perceive the things which may be beneficial to your education. Open your ears children and listen carefully to what is being said, probably you may hear a piece of an advice, which might save you from the pitfall." *Therefore, with respect to what has been mentioned above, good parents are those who pay attention to any question which has been raised by a child, even thought the question might sound as being a trivial nonsense; however, it could possibly be a mind-blowing to a wise parent or adult.* **In this case, children's questions and actions help parents to develop the process of child education based on their immediate needs or aspiration.**

PARENTS SEIZED ANOTHER OPPORTUNITY TO CLARIFY THE ISSUE OF INCEST TO THE INNOCENT CHILDREN, WHO APPEARED COMPLETELY ALERT AND READY TO LEARN.

Parents therefore, had seized this opportunity to begin educating the children regarding the topic of **"INCEST."** Zuka's mother began saying, son, "Asala is your sister! Please remember from this day on, **Brothers and Sisters can never get married**, because you possess the **same blood (the same mother and the same father)**." Mrs. Kayalu continued, "*Such thing is against the law of ancestors. It is strictly forbidden before our Nzambe (our*

Great God.). Your sister, Asala would have to get married to another fellow, born from a different family.

Further, the man that Asala would marry will have to come from a different family." Zuka, his father added, "When you will grow up, the woman you will have to marry will have to be born from a different family from Zuka and Asala's parents. This means that she will have a different mother and father.

Zuka again asked, "**Why Papa**?" The father replied, "Well, because of the sake of your children." *We will continue to gradually teach you many things regarding this subject and many more. So do not worry about knowing everything now."* *Eventually, parents will continue to touch this subject as well as many other sensitive areas until the children reach the age of maturity.*

He continued, both of you should therefore know that, a husband does not call his wife, **Mama, unless,** he loves his wife so dearly that he could occasionally, call her Mama. However, in this context, it has another implication. *It simply means,* **darling,** *or the mother of my beloved children.* Technically, the wife does not call her husband **Papa**, unless, she also wants to express a high degree of her love to the father of her beloved children; in that case, it has also another connotation; *it implies the word, darling.* However, this is not a norm in our society, and it only happens rarely. And therefore, a brother and a sister **Can Never Get Married nor Have Children**!" The mother insisted on that fact.

Finally, she questioned them, "Zuka and Asala do you understand now? This fact would be extremely wrong. This is a **_HUGE problem_** in our Bantu culture; and they call this situation "**Incest**."

Also, remember that a child born through incest relationship is undervalued in our society, because our Great Being, God does not permit our ancestors to honor such a filthy thing, because it is wrong. In our Christian religion, we say, "That is a **Sin**!"

Asala, Mrs. Kayalu said to her daughter, "This instruction applies to you, as well. Please remember that when you will grow up, *the man you shall marry must be born from different parents*. That man will have to have a different mother and father from yours. He will have to come from different family as well. You must remember that always." Mr. and Mrs. Kayalu warned their children about the danger of having children from **Incest Relationship**.

Children were told explicitly the consequences of producing an offspring from incest relationship, that, "it was actually an anomaly practice. Further, such a child would exhibit a higher degree of inconsistency in his or her behavior, because their parents have been defiant to the law of our Nzambe, or our Great God, as well as to the law of our ancestors. Therefore, our society cannot tolerate such an awful view; and the parents of those children would be underestimated in the eyes of everyone in the entire world." Kayalu's children had the privilege to receive such education since their younger age. They had learned the nuance between a sister and brother and also that between a husband and his wife.

Highlighting Appropriate Manners

ADRESSING PROPER BEHAVIOR

As we have previously discussed, the process of child education in the Bantu/Congolese culture is actually based on observation, because there is no pre defined rules. The incident below had urged both parents to address the topic of appropriate behavior among children.

Apparently, the boy (Zuka) appeared aggressive compared to the girl (Asala) who appeared passive. The mother had given two Mikate (donuts) to each child. After finishing eating his second donut, the boy (Zuka) was about to seize his sister's second donut, who had the habit of eating too slow. All of a sudden, Asala shouted at her brother,"No, Zuka, you have just eaten your second donut. Stop, this one is mine, do not take it!" Meantime, Zuka had already cut a piece of Asala's Mikate (donut); so, noticing her brother inconsiderate action, Asala got annoyed, and spilled some water at her brother's head. Suddenly, this resulted to a fight, between both children. Observation of this sad scenario had permitted their parents to educate the children concerning SELFISHNESS, VIOLENCE AND RESPECT.

With respect to addressing social behavior, Mangeli and Ezombo taught their children, the suitable manners of addressing family members or siblings.

Besides from Mama and Papa, the appropriate approach of addressing siblings is to follow the natural **hierarchy** among the children. The older child must be addressed as "**Yaya,**" this is a title of respect in Lingala and Kikongo language for instance, and it actually means Great or Big brother or big sister.

Further." Mrs. Kayalu added, "Remember children when you address somebody as "Yaya," you cannot cross the line. Every single word you address to "Yaya" must entail nothing but respect, because she or he had seen the **Sun of** this Earth before you did!"Furthermore, when you want everything to belong to you alone, that is selfishness, and that is absolutely wrong. Also, know that when you begin fighting or spilling water at each other, that is called violence, that is socially unacceptable. Our ancestors had thought us a Big word called R E S P E C T, in Lingala language we said, "**BOTOSI** (bohtohsee), in Kikongo language, we said, **LUZITU** (louzeetu).

The mother had seized this opportunity to inculcate the magnitude of the word RESPECT which is practiced in their Bantu/Congolese culture, to her two children. The father finally underlined the following words; "Children remember **Selfishness**, **Violence**, **Stealing** and **Lethargy** are not your ancestors' values. Therefore, do not attempt to practice them as long as you shall live in this world, because they dishonor our Nzambe or Nzambi-Mpungu – The Great Being in heaven. He is not pleased when we misbehave. Therefore, we ought to fear *HIS ANGER.*"

Children Behaviors at Home as well as in the Society

How a well bred Congolese child should reply to his or her parents or to their big brothers/sisters (or Yaya), whenever he or she is called?

Mrs. Mr. Kayalu told their children: "When one of the parents calls you, you ought to reply spontaneously in the following manner: for example, if you hear your name being called, "**Zuka!**" You should immediately reply, "**Mama or Papa or Yaya**"

to whoever is calling you at that time, or you can be an extra polite by adding, "Yes, mama", or "Yes, Papa." Please remember henceforth that, a well bred Congolese child is never allowed to answer to his parents or Yaya or any elderly person with the word "***WHAT!***" This is absolutely not an acceptable term as far as our Congolese culture is concerned. Such a word is regarded to be **DISRESPECTFUL** in the Bantu/Congolese society. In fact, in Lingala language the word WHAT is translated as, "NINI" (ne-ne) and in KIKONGO language is translated as "NKI (uhn-Ke) both ways, sound very harsh to the listeners. Therefore, the usage of the word "What" in the Bantu/Congolese culture implies anger, pejorative word. The parents of any kid using the word "WHAT" when called are criticized indeed for having failed to educate the child appropriately since its formative years.

Furthermore, as far as addressing other family members such as uncles and grandparents, children, you must address them by their respective **title,** followed by their first names in order to be specific, should there be more than one of them at that same location and also, at that particular time. You should know that uncle is called "Noko" in Lingala language or Ngwasi (uhn-gouase) in Kikongo language, and oncle in French. Grandparents should be addressed as "**Koko**" in Lingala language or **Nkak**a (uhn-Kah-kah) in Kikongo language, and grandPère or grandMère in French. Again, their first names could be added to specify the name.

However, outside of the immediate family, children should address any person who appears to be in the range of their father's or mother's age, by prefacing that

individual's name with the title "**Tata**" (referring to a **male individual (Mr.)** or "**Mama**" (referring to a **female individual (Mrs.**) or Monsieur ou Madame in French, example, Tata Mupinga (meaning Mr. Mupinga), Mama Mupinga (meaning Mrs. Mupinga or Monsieur or Madame Mupinga. In fact, using those titles, in this context "Tata and Mama" followed by somebody's name signifies just Mr. and Mrs. That actually had nothing to do with the titles of immediate parents. Therefore, a well bred Congolese child is definitely not permitted to address an adult by his or her first or last name, because this would be regarded as a derogatory attitude.

The first questions the community members would be asking, "Those children have been educated by whom?" Naturally, the children's parents cannot get any credit for the naughty behaviors of their children in the society.

Child Safety

How Do Congolese Parents Walk With Their Children on the Street?

In order to ensure children safety, Congolese parents instruct their children that when walking on the street, they must always remember to walk before their parents. If they are walking parallel however, a child should be holding parents' hands for a security reason. Children are not permitted to remain behind a grown up, because parents feel insecure to do so. They deem necessary to place them forward, and watch them closely as they walk; and then, be geared up to assist them at any wrong movement, or in the attempt to touch any harmful object. Thus, placing a child forward is safer than allowing him or her to be walking behind.

Further, it is safer, because a guardian or parents do not actually have another pair of eyes behind their heads to be able to notice whether or not the kid had made any deviation, which may result to any negative outcomes. So, it is preferable to become aware of all those details in order to prevent any type of dilemma.

Furthermore, leaving the kid behind is considered to be hazardous, because the child could also be picked up by any stranger; who could easily harm the innocent kid, without that adult knowing anything in that regard. In fact, this is a reason why an African mother proves to be so protective of her child. She would prefer to rather carry her child on her back instead of allowing any person, whom she feels uncomfortable or suspicious to babysit her infant. This is the main reason why an African woman has always been portrayed carrying a child on her back. Such illustration is indeed to exemplify the safety motive.

CHILD SAFETY MEASURES

It is vitally important for an adult to walk closely with a child, and it is preferable for an adult to grip the child's hand in order to ensure the kid's safety on the road. The picture below depicts a proper approach of walking with a child on the street. It shows a Grandma walking along with her granddaughter on the street. This actually confirms the fact that Congolese parents are so protective of their children. When accompanying a youngster, Princess Wanjo Maboye feels that grasping the kid's hand is safer, because she is in full control of that child's movement. Further she is viewing every step the youngster is making, so, the child cannot touch any harmful substance or object while walking with her grandma on the road.

CHILD SAFETY: WALKING WITH A CHILD ON THE ROAD

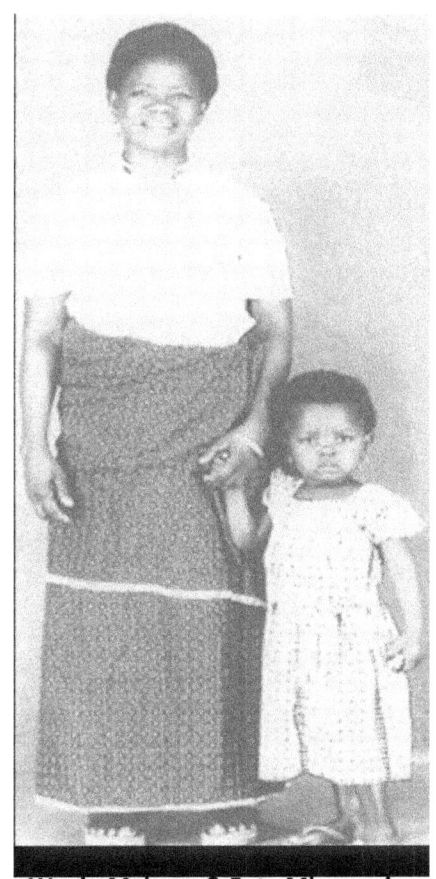

Wanjo Maboye & Fota Mbayami
Grandmother & her Granddaughter

Congolese Parents believe that it would be much safer to hold a child's hand when walking with it on the street in order to prevent any hazardous occurrences.

Chapter 3

Contrasting Activities of Urban vs. Rural areas Students

This picture illustrates the performance of Junior High School Students in Kinshasa, on Campus ground. Parents and guests attend the performance, at least twice a year.

This picture depicts Education in the Rural Areas due to poor leadership

In the rural areas, learning conditions are very difficult. These children, some of them walk miles to get to Mission Schools in order to attend school on a regular basis; nevertheless, they are willing to invest their efforts and their time to commute. On the other hand, their families are willing to invest the little income they own in their children's education, because they want to ensure a better future for their kids.

Contrasting Activities of Urban Students vs. Rural Students

This picture depicts: Celebration of the city Governor's birthday held outdoors at Athenée Square, by all the high schools students of the city of Kinshasa, the Capital city of the Congo RDC.

High School Students in Kinshasa, the City Capital Performing Western dance

Elementary School Kids – In the Rural area

This picture depicts: Elementary School kids in the rural area, scattered here and there during break time.

In general, children begin their primary education at the age of six. Usually, from this time the kids who come from well to do families had already mastered the most important basic subjects, such as Math, Reading and Writing. Around the age of six also, children begin learning the singing activities. They sing religious songs mostly, and learn to say short prayers prior to beginning class instructions, also, prior to going to bed, and shortly upon awakening in the morning. In addition, before eating their meals, children are also taught to be grateful for their daily meals by reciting a short prayer for the blessing of the food, as well as blessing the cook, usually "Mama."

Parents are also compelled to teach their children the importance of attending school on a regular basis. Kids are also advised to study well and do their homework, diligently in order to receive good grades and keep up with this spirit. Apparently, children who keep on bringing good report cards home, which contain excellent marks, are sometimes given some incentive, because they make their families cheerful. They themselves feel good about it, and they are motivated to go forwards.

Generally, those are the kids who come from the well to do families. Usually, their parents have taken the initiative of teaching them how to read and write from home, way before attending school, beginning at the early days. They also, have learned how to say their daily prayers of various occasions, as opposed to those who have not been privileged to learn how to read and write from home, or how to say their prayers, due to the fact that they have come from modest or poor families. These kids, usually, when they first attend school, they experience such a hard time to grasp the most basic courses or the most important subjects such as Math, Reading and Writing. These kids truly face a lot of challenges in terms of catching up with the most privileged children. They, initially appear timid around the most advanced children. Nevertheless, they struggle in doing their best, and gradually they overcome their shyness; sometimes, however, they excel.

One may in fact, notice some degree of difference and similarity between the Congolese children who are raised in the rural areas compared to those who had been reared in the urban areas, so to speak. Ordinarily, Congolese mothers, whether they are established in the rural areas, or those living in the urban areas, most of them prefer initiating their daughters in culinary activities so that they could learn how to prepare different types of national dishes. Habitually, they begin from the age of 12 and on. In fact, while they are on vacation or after school, most girls look forward to assisting their mothers in kitchen areas. Most of them have developed a high degree of desire to learn cooking, and therefore, they are eager to experiment their ability to master the preparation of those dishes.

In the rural areas however, girls do much more than those in the urban areas. The students from elementary school, and those from junior high schools, who live off Mission campus, do extra work in assisting parents with house chores. Apparently, those kids are aware of the types of tasks that are required around the house. They become conscious of the manners in which they should go about prioritizing those duties in order to better assist their parents. And therefore, the child would just go ahead and perform that duty without waiting to receive any order or instructions from his or her parents to assist in that routine.

Illustration on page 65 portrays an eight-year-old boy, out of his volition, decides to bring drinking water in the house. Upon his return from school, he realized that there was no drinking water in their home. On his own volition, his first reaction is to take a bucket; and then, fearlessly, would go to the water fountain, which may be located half a mile away from home in order to get spring water, and bring it to his parents' home.

This is actually how the parents had begun training their son. The boy is growing with a sense of responsibility. He already knows how to take initiatives at his early age; and this implies that this child will grow to become independent or self- sufficient as soon as he reaches the stage of adulthood. Further, the boy proves that he will set a good example in the society by becoming a hard-working man, as well as being a self-sufficient individual.

In addition, this boy will eventually become an excellent provider for his future family. This is an indication that this boy would make a positive contribution in the future to the society. This actually is where an African man's responsibilities really begin.

Further, the students in the rural areas exert their energy in walking back and forth, and that is, from Monday through Friday, and from Mission schools to their villages. Besides, they have also developed the habit of assisting their folks in many various activities, right after school such as cultivating their parents' fields, or in getting involved in the farming activities. In addition, some of the kids are engaged in various activities such as fixing fish ponds and exercising pisciculture work, and that including fishing, whereas children whom parents are producers of pottery, acquire direct experience in that area such as assisting in gathering clay from the source designed to make pottery. They get excited in learning how to mold, or shape moist clay. They follow the process of making pottery carefully such as hardening and heating it to the point where they are able to produce a variety of objects such as pots, vases, tea kettles, a huge bottle designed to keep the water pure and cool.

Certainly, rural children, due to the fact that they exercise all the physical activities mentioned above, they gradually grow in building confidence, as well as in acquiring the ability to master serious responsibilities. Boys are told since their younger age that lazy men are unwanted by women, as well as by our Bantu society. In fact, nobody actually values them, until they decide to adopt a positive attitude towards life, and then become productive; that is when they can actually gain respect.

Relationship between Congolese Parents and Their Children

Basically, the desire to assist parents comes spontaneously to all the African children. They do not expect any reward from their parents. It is likewise for their parents, never will they attempt to make any types of deals with their children such as reimbursing the money which they had spent for their education. In fact such deals would actually sound peculiar to the Bantu/Congolese culture. In essence, the acknowledgement of their obligations towards their children is innate to African parents. The Congolese children do always remember their parents in such a natural way. Generally, children believe that it is their primary duties to render all the necessary services required to their parents. As a matter of fact, they would do it without any reservation.

In addition, children realize that such services represent merely a token of gratitude for all the necessary efforts parents had made in providing them a loving care, which had brought them forth this far. Therefore, all the services are done joyously, harmoniously without whining while taking such an approach. This explains how much African children remained committed to their loving parents, and that, until they leave this world.

Because they remember that parents had nurtured them with a very serious discipline, and also with a lot of love, patience, as well as compassion. Further, they had endeavored to shape them until to the point where they have become educated or scholars. Certainly African parents do not get into any type of contract with their children. So, whatever they do or give to their kids, it is actually done out of unconditional love. The children also, respond naturally to that love by being grateful. We can therefore conclude that the interaction between African parents and their children is somewhat reciprocal, so to speak.

AGRICULTURE ACTIVITIES

ORGANIC VEGETABLE

In the rural areas fathers are eager to get theirs sons involved in agriculture activities.

Mr. Lokombo is watering Matembele vegetable. His children usually come after school to water this vegetable garden. They have been trained how to pull out the weeds. Mr. Lokombo and his children have such a cooperative action. He began training his children since their childhood. They have no problem in getting involved with such duties.

EMBRACING INITIATIVES: Kikesa Puita, Eight Years Old

An Elementary Student from a Rural Area

After school, he decides to help his parents by going to the water fountain in order to get water and bring it home. He begins taking his responsibility at his early

Kikesa Puita is a very diligent boy. As soon as he returns from school, he notices that there is no drinking water in the house.

Therefore, he does not need to be reminded to take his bucket and go to the water fountain in order to get water and bring it to his parents.

This boy will grow up with a sense of responsibility of his own life, and that of his future family.

He will never become a beggar or a swindler in his life, but self-sufficient. Further, **Puita** will contribute positively in the Congolese society.

Chapter 4

A Learning Process (Girls' Duties)

Girls are eager to start learning how to make different types of the Bantu peoples 'dishes, such as preparing Fufu, Pondu, Fish, Mbika (Pumpkin Seed), Beans, Chicken as well as different types of vegetables (**Read Africa presents the Congo, RDC and Congolese Cuisine**), usually girls are permitted to prepare these dishes in a very small quantity; initially, it is done on a trial basis.

Basically, this learning process is very challenging to most Congolese girls who fall between the ages of ten to twelve. They usually experience a series of trial and errors. The process is actually meant to go gradually, because at the beginning, certainly, they do not always get their first cooking right. For instance, the preparation of the Fufu is a very big thing for inexperienced person. At the beginning, most of the time, to unskillful candidate, ninety per cent of the time, does not get it right, because it comes out bad.

Obviously, this fact appears amusing to the grown up around the family cycle. However, to any the girl who are striving to get it right, so that she could earn some credits from Mom and Dad or siblings, this seems to be a very frustrating experience indeed. Sometimes, the girl would wind up crying to satisfy her frustrations, especially when the adults start mocking her cooking experience. However, parents who had gone through similar childhood experiences understand the situations immediately; and are prompt to console their daughters. In fact, family members encourage the girls to keep

on trying, until they would ultimately get it right in the future, eventually. Apparently, they do get it right as time goes by with a lot of practice. By the time a Congolese girl reaches the age of fourteen years old, usually, she had mastered the cooking of the main dishes. In addition, at that age, she has also mastered the art of arranging or fixing things around the house; for instance, doing dishes, washing clothes, ironing, sweeping floors, and dusting furniture and even babysitting.

    Furthermore, contrasting between boys raised in the urban areas, and those who have been nurtured in the rural areas, one can actually conclude that those who have been raised in the rural regions are more knowledgeable in terms of maintenance, and handling of the responsibilities around the family. It has been noticed that the ability of the rural boys excelled that of the urban boys. The boys in the rural areas gradually learn almost all the physical work such as helping out around the farms, and learning how to make or create fish ponds for the breeding of various types of fishes. Further, the rural boys also learn how to make fishing nets or tools and its activities, including the breeding of the cattle, or the raising of fowls, opposed to urban kids.

    Additionally, the young men are taught the trading activities. They begin doing it within their own county first, and subsequently, they can extend travelling in bordered countries. Therefore, the children who are raised in the rural areas, most of them, matured faster, and they grow to be very hard- working people compare to those children who had grown up in the urban areas, in the Democratic Republic of Congo.

In contrast, both gender, whether girls or boys who have been raised in the urban areas, and especially, those who come from well to do families, learn in moderation, because in general, their families provide domestics to work around their homes. They also are supplied the means of transportation, including a chauffeur to drive them, back and forth to school. A well to do family also provides gardeners as well as security guards around their property. These kids are exposed to a high standard of living with less or no pressure compare to other kids. And therefore, these details leave a minor work for some boys growing in the urban areas to do, base on the environment where they are raised. This actually explains the difference between the urban and rural Congolese children in terms of their school education, as well as their abilities to master situations around themselves, or in the society in general.

Additionally, by observation, the urban teenagers who have abruptly lost their folks, experience an awfully hard time trying to just and to cope with life's responsibilities, whereas those in the rural environments, due to long habit they had already formed by working along with their parents since their younger age, adapt easily to such change, which is really regarded as a continuation of their daily activities.

Moreover, the experience of the children who had been raised in the urban areas, and who have come from the well to do families in Africa, is quite different from that of those reared in the remote parts of the countries. Apparently, when both group of individuals travel abroad, and are suddenly exposed to the harsh living conditions in a foreign land, those who are raised in rural area cope much better, reportedly.

ACTIVITIES *IN THE RURAL AREAS*

PARENTS ALSO EXPOSE THEIR CHILDREN WHO HAVE REACHED THE AGE OF TWELVE YEARS OLD TO THE FIELD WORK ESPECIALLY THOSE CHILDRENWHO HATE SCHOOL.

Cassava Field is tilled in many different regions of the Congo RDC: Girls are trained in this area. In general, everyone gets involved in producing cassava, but in some areas women and their daughters are the major producers. Therefore, girls must make sure that they actually learn every step required to cultivate cassava, when they decide to settle in the rural areas. This topic is vitally important.

A Young Man is fishing at his Parents' Fish Pond.

This is one of the many activities which the young people are engaged in the rural areas in order to develop their future responsibilities.

In exercising their African's men stamina, in the rural areas, the young men get involved in making fish ponds which is designed for fish breeding activities; they usually work along with their parents. The fish ponds are the ideal means of acquiring fresh fish at will, and at any time they choose to eat a fresh fish.

Cultural Education

Generally, by the end of their sixth grade, an African student has acquired almost all the general knowledge regarding their culture such as the knowledge of their own tribes, including all the necessary details involved such as their Province, Sectors, District, and the villages where their parents were actually born.

Parents are required to reveal the names of their great-grandparents' or great-uncles in order to ensure their origin. The youth also learn family structure, whether their families practice patrilineal or matrilineal system.

Additionally, they find it important to mention their families' background; whether they had been common people in the past, or elite who came from one of those various Kongo kingdoms. Furthermore, parents are obligated to disclose to the children, the government structure of their village, for instance: *who governs the village? What qualifications should an individual have in order to become a chief in his native village?*

Why should a village chief always come from the ancient royal family? Further parents ought to reveal to the children that this is

not a simple matter. It is rather a complex issue, because any usurper of this power should always be brought to the Traditional Court of law for his implication in such crime (Please read, Africa presents the Congo RDC and Traditional law.)

Basically, as it was previously indicated, concerning "Child Education, it is the father's duty to explain to his son (s) what to expect when he will become a mature man.

Likewise, the mother's duty is to highlight the necessary facts required in female life; or what to expect when the girl reaches the maturity age. Should both parents be deceased, in that case, the responsibilities of rearing a child, or children would fall on their immediate relatives such as uncles and aunts, or on any other extended family members. The most important thing is to have the children rooted in their traditions.

Regarding spiritual development, Congolese parents, ensure to reveal a high degree of spiritual understanding to their children, contrasting both traditional religions versus Christian religion. Historically speaking, parents also explain to the youth, how **"Nzambi-Mpungu"** (God Almighty) was recognized and adored by their ancestors, even prior to the arrival of the early catholic missionaries. *In addition, folks should explain the main reason why a great number of African or Congolese people including their children continue to remain pagans up to these days,* *and yet spiritual revival has been growing daily throughout the country.*

The short answer to this question would be, "**The reasons why some Africans, or Congolese people in particular continue to remain pagans up to the present time, is due to the skepticism or the mistrust of the early missionaries' intrigues**. In fact, according to the oral traditions, it has been revealed that prior to the arrival of the early, so called missionaries, in the Kingdom of Kongo, the King of Kongo (Congo) had always exemplified his majestic power over his Kingdom. He was capable to oversee all the situations involved in the land, and that including ensuring the safety of his people in such a meticulously manners.

However, the King of Kongo's interaction with Catholic missionaries had caused an appalling relationship between both parties, in the name of God. The fact that the King provided his African's hospitality in good faith, his trust was taken as frailness. This had actually been the beginning of the dreadful African history of the Bantu/Congolese people. Because, of the Catholic missionaries' diplomacy, the church was able to succeed its scheme. As a result, the King of the kingdom of the Kongo lost control over the land, and evidently, he could no longer ensure the safety of his constituents. His frailty caused him to lose his power. Eventually, he succumbed to Catholic missionaries' temptation. Apparently having a wrong motive deep down in their hearts, missionaries took advantage of the King, his people, as well as that of the land including its resources. Instead of bringing peace and harmony to the people, the practice of religion became nothing, but diplomatic conspiracy. Consequently, a peaceful society was replaced by missionaries' insecurity where family members had been forcibly separated from their loved ones under the guise of religion or friendship. Ultimately such intolerable activities had resulted to all kind of frustrations, mistrust or skepticism to any types of missionaries' activities.

The above mentioned facts are apparently the reasons why many individuals in the Bantu society of Congo RDC choose to remain pagans up to these days. ***They argue that they do not see any evidence that would convince them that the later missionaries' activities are opposite of the ones that were exhibited by the early missionaries. This is where the unbelievers come from. Further, this is the area where the new missionaries meet their serious challenges in terms of evangelization.***

Apparently, there is a spiritual battle nowadays, so to speak. We estimate that the only type of missionaries that can be successful in winning souls from this tough area would only be those missionaries who are really anointed. And who can exemplify the Power of the Living God. The Tent Makers or those similar to the earlier missionaries would not be able to make it. In fact, attempting to take this approach would not be recommended. It would actually be unsafe, because individuals who are rooted in their firm pagan beliefs continue to argue, especially when they begin to compare the previous facts from the present such as the economic development which the State of Kongo had reached prior to the arrival of catholic missionaries in terms of trading and manufacturing of goods with the disasters which the land has been exposed to nowadays, they perceive nothing but cynicism.

This comparison, certainly strengthens their incredibility, and increases their skepticism in missionary's activities. These individuals have always been suspicious of foreign religion, because they feel that it is nothing but the continuation of the early missionaries' scheme. They confirm, "We were better off prior to their arrival in our land. Their presence had made us worse off. They took us from the top where we have been self-sufficient and have driven us way to the tail where we have now become dependent upon others. Didn't we actually fail to listen to our ancestors' advice? Why should our youth continue to be perished, and not be able to utilize their African's man stamina? Why shouldn't they be able to acquire whatever they need at will?

Obviously, the presence of the usurpers in our land had been detrimental to us. Why should our youth succumb to such snare, and eventually be attempted to make similar mistake which King Nzinga-Nkuvu had made in the name of foreign religion which does not fear the Power of our Nzambe, our Great Being from Heaven the one that can strike over everyone or everything that is defiant? And yet, even our little gods fear our Nzambe greatly. We do not see any apparent reason that can attract our attention to listen to those individuals, despite of their few inducements.

In fact, while the majority discuss this issue covertly, the most aggressive individuals among them had said it overtly, especially when they perceive missionary's activities in progress, they said, "This scenario has been going on for decades now in our land, and yet we notice no positive effects from it, except the increase of negativity in every sector; so how can we possibly be convinced by all these various activities which seek to blind our people perpetually, as well as conceal our values?

Evidently, it is up to the parents, really to ensure the clarity of this matter, and elaborate the cause of certain modern social issues which continue to prevail at the present time. Sometimes, parents whisper in the children' ears regarding what really happened in the past, and why such situation really occurred? And who are their authors?

Certainly, in regard to oral traditions, parents, grandparents, and/or great-grandparents are considered to be family's live Historians, because everything they report is factual. Therefore, the youth would have to refer to it with reverence. In fact, when the earlier missionaries entered the Kingdom of Kongo, certainly, they did misrepresent the Christian religion to the King of the kingdom of Kongo and his people; who ignorantly trusted them wholeheartedly. Apparently, their true motive was at first concealed in the attempt to gain his complete trust, and so that they could do damage to his kingdom afterward. All those activities were being actually done cunningly. In reality, however, their inner motive was deceitful.

Consequently, many families lost their loved ones abruptly, with no slighted idea of their whereabouts. Such atrocity had occurred in the sake of baptism and especially religion which was brought to the King of Kongo, by the early missionaries. Pagans mock it, and put all kind of pejorative labels over it in the attempt to discourage people from welcoming missionaries in the land. However, the anointed servants of God, through revival are winning their victories.

The new generation always wonders, "What types of baptism did the King received?" The answer is, "*Whether it had been by immersion in the water, or by sprinkling of the water upon his head, nevertheless, that political or religious relationship with strangers, had in some degree left family members both, from the root or the mother land and those across the ocean-heartbroken.*" On one hand, those who had remained in the root or the mother land continue to mourn their loved one who had been forcibly taken across the ocean sneakily, or otherwise. The family members of the victims had developed all sorts of imaginary things their minds.

Some among them believed that their loved ones were probably killed and their bodies were turned to canned meat by the profits individuals. As a result, many Congolese people had just refused to eat canned meat which was termed in Bandundu region, as "*ELENGEYE (ah-lay-uhn-gah-yay)*". People used to whisper in each other's ears," **DO NOT BUY, OR EVEN EAT THE CANNED MEAT.**" It appears suspicious.

It had neither a label nor an expiration date. Another thing, people could not identify the origin of this product; whether the manufacturer's name, or the country from where it was being canned. That crucial information was omitted.

People brought all kinds of speculations regarding this product. "Who knows, they said, "That canned meat may possibly be *my robust uncle "Tuntwa" or my aunt "Lutala" or it could as well be the flesh body of my cousin Mupia who had been kidnapped by foreign merchants*. It could also be your own family members in those cans, they said to each other in order to discourage people from buying it. It was being reported that, "The individuals who actually eat that meat, were developing skin rash." Some kept on expressing their concerns in various manners such as, "Who really knows the truth about this political-religious dilemma? " Since the ancestors had gone, we have been left behind without any proper guidance, with deep recurring regret. The King and his kingdom had failed us utterly without any compunction.

In essence, concerning that suspicious unhealthy canned meat, various individuals began reporting their findings, one person had said, ***"I perceived a part of a human chin with beard attached to it inside the can, as soon as I had opened "ELENGEYE (ahlan-ga-yah) Canned meat." Another individual had reported seeing, "A human finger including a nail attached to it in the canned meat he had bought, and then I discarded it."*** Several other individuals had reported many related awful incidents in that regard. This product actually sparked fear. It aroused anger in many people. Evidently, the population especially in Luniungu Sector of Bandundu Province, was outraged to experience and also to hear some of these negative reports regarding the so called. *ELENGEYE canned meat.* Apparently, they became resentful of their leaders who had exemplified such a poor leadership for allowing the import of unhealthy food in the country; besides, it was the food which nobody knew its origin. Who was to blame? The people to blame were really the early Catholic missionaries who began deceitful activities, as well as the King of the kingdom of Kongo himself, who had not exemplified his ancestors' wisdom, apparently the inducement rendered him frail to the point where he could not utilize his God's given discernment.

Apparently, because of the incitation of his guests, the King had lost his insight to perceive long ahead. He was unfortunately unable to sense the upcoming danger.

Obviously, he was distracted by the outside priests' appearance. The youth would infer however, that the practice of King Nzinga-Nkuvu's African hospitality had let the door wide open to embrace the foe in his land. Probably, such was the beginning of the African Continent's miseries which resulted to slavery, colonial exploitation, violence, brain washing of the people, as well as the distortion of the African's history and values. It is appalling indeed to notice that all these mischievous motives could continue to be justified by a Religious Institution (Catholic Church in such a cunningly manners). Because we are dealing with historical facts, it is therefore, necessary to gradually expose them to every child in order to raise its self-awareness as it moves slowly in the path of child education.

In fact, in Bandundu Province, where this canned meat was introduced in a very large scale, in order to boycott that suspicious product, a group of local musicians were inspired to some degree, and composed a song which became so popular in the area. It was to degrade the product completely. *The lyric was as follow: "People beware eating that canned meat, because it is causing severe skin rash. Our loved ones are disappearing from left to right. Who really knows their whereabouts? Skin rash is being erupted due to the consumption of "Elengeye "canned meat. Could that be a sign to alert everyone that, we should "STOP! "You are probably eating your own family members who had been kidnapped by the invaders, by the impostors and by those foreigner traders!" STOP!*

Since those individuals have no regret to feed us unhealthy food. ELENGEYE canned meat could as well be a BIG DOG! Who knows, oh who knows? ***SO DISCONTINUE BUYING, OR EATING IT, RIGHT NOW!" THIS ACTUALLY WAS SABOTAGE! Eventually shortly after that time, the product had vanished from the market, because no one was buying it anymore. Apparently, the power of Nzambe (uhn-Zah-mbah) – The Great Being from heaven, by His grace had saved His people from such confusions.***

However, since families were abruptly separated, those who remained in the mother Land had developed a high degree of disdain against missionaries and their religious activities, which had caused the rupture of families' joy, which ultimately had been replaced with bitterness between both parts. Because of the earliest missionaries' deceitfulness, the pagans continue to show resistance in accepting the true gospel of Jesus Christ. They go on remaining skeptical due to that bitterness, as was previously indicated.

Besides from the deceitful and negative influence from the early catholic missionaries which had left the King of Kongo powerless, several students both elementary as well as high school, throughout the country, had undergone awful or atrocious experiences at the Catholic Mission Campus. Kids had involuntarily been directed to the practice of ungodly stuff. And yet, parents had always trusted that Mission schools students would receive a better education both intellectually as well as spiritually. Apparently, this has not been the case. Many kids have been exposed to the ungodly world under the guise of revealing to them a special teaching, which would make them become very intelligent, more powerful; very wealthy, successful, and influentially sound during their life time." (Ref. please read "**RESCAPE DE L'ENFER**" French version **ISBN 2-909100-00-6)** by *Bakajika Muana Nkuba*, in order to confirm the fact mentioned above, and yet such teaching has been very detrimental to those African youth. However, God by His mercy is saving one by one through spiritual revival, brought forth by anointed servants of the Living God.

The African new generation and especially the Congolese children, conclude sadly that – the frailty of the King had disqualified his leadership, on one hand. And on the other hand, however, being a King who had been enthroned based on his high ancient qualifications and merit, if the King had really known that the earlier missionaries were not afraid of their "**NZAMBE/NZAMBI-MPUNGU** (*GOD THE ALMIGHTY* of the Universe)" the king would have been reluctant to accept such religious ceremony, which had weaken his kingdom, and also endanger his constituents.

According to the oral traditions, the early missionaries were never invited by the King of the kingdom of Kongo.(Nzinga Nkuvu). They actually came on their own volition, apparently pretending to establish a harmonious or peaceful diplomatic and spiritual relationship which unfortunately resulted to a nightmare.

Children should bear in mind that the relationship between Portugal and the Kingdom of Kongo was established through Diego Cao who was a Portuguese explorer. He was a diplomatic and a seeming spiritual liaison between both countries. It is necessary to mention that the Kingdom of Kongo was known to be a highly developed State in terms of trading- network by the time the Portuguese entered the land. The country traded diverse goods such as Natural resources and Ivory. The State of Kongo also manufactured and traded pottery and copperware.

With respect to the religious ceremony, clearly being an African leader, the King knew nothing concerning baptism, and therefore, he was not the one who requested to be baptized, because he was anchored in his ancestral beliefs and especially the belief in his NZAMBI-MPUNGU (uhn-Zahmbe-uhm-Pungu), God the Great Being who resides high in heaven. Because catholic priests or the early missionaries were the ones who brought the word, "Baptism", they actually persuaded the King and his people to accept the new religion through baptism.

Apparently, he did it in good faith, (according to our Oral traditions). However, if the King of Kongo had really known that those catholic priests were not genuine servants of God, and that attempting to establish trade between Portugal and Kongo would create more miseries rather than a peaceful relationship, certainly, there would have been a strong resistance, which could have prevented a negative outcome to our contemporary African history.

Additionally, when the early missionaries arrived in the Kingdom of Kongo, they noticed the splendor of the ancient Kongo kingdom. They also perceived the solidarity and the cultural unity of the people in that land. Further, The State of Kongo was highly developed in terms of trading, as it was previously indicated. As far as spiritual development is concerned, the people of Kingdom of Kongo were quite aware of the existence of the Great Being in Heaven whose power was invincible. That being is called Nzambe in Lingala language or Nzambi-Mpungu in Kikongo language, or Mungu in Swahili.

Nevertheless, because of the new Era, Spiritual revival has been so powerful in the mind of many Congolese people. As a result, some illumined Congolese parents have acquired different view in this matter. Therefore, they are urging the younger generation to bear in mind that, "Every human being is fallible, regardless to his or her social rank! And therefore, it is preferable to learn, and view things objectively, also try not to dwell in situations which can no longer be remedied."

Further, folks continue to advise their children as follow, "Know that the love of "Nzambe-Mpungu" (God Almighty, the King of the Universe is so powerful. It is able to dissolve and consume all the past bitterness. It would be preferable if everyone would take his or her own responsibilities in life, and that, without seeking to rationalize awful events, or attempting to portray them positively when they have actually been indecent.

Currently, however, those parents who have acquired some degree of spiritual illumination understand their obligations towards their children, and also to their family members, who are still dwelling in the past social issues, or those who are still caught into rejection, bitterness and resentment feelings. It is worthy reminding everyone that there is a perfect solution to that dilemma.

Because of our ancestors' devotion and acknowledgement of our Nzambe Mpungu, the Great God, a Congolese religion called Kimbaguist, named after its leader emerged in the early 1920s.. Nzambe or God bestowed a spiritual gift to Simon Kimbangu. He received a divine call and visions to preach the word of God, exemplifying the power of the living God to his people. His mission was to illumine his people, and guide them in practicing of monotheism, rather than focusing in little gods, in the practice of fetishes, sorcery, magic, charms, witches, as well as the desire to performing polygamy. His doctrine was convincing; he healed by the laying on of hands. His doctrine was different from that of the early missionaries. Apparently, the colonial masters felt threatened to witness the Power of the living God through this man.

They feared that the oppressed people would become illumined, courageous and rebellious, which would limit the colonial power to dominate them further, consequently, Prophet Simon Kimbangi was sentenced and put to death under the guide of being a false prophet, according to the oral traditions. Nevertheless Kimbanguist religion had not ended. It had spread throughout the nation. That is a gift of Spiritual Revival, which is not originated from any earthly individual, but the Nzambe Himself, and therefore it would be wise seeking his grace. It is given to everyone who wants to be set completely free, because it brings understanding to the human mind. It helps clarify that the world and all upon it is still imperfect. Heaven alone is perfect.

Additionally, condemnatory attitude is nothing, but a spiritual immaturity. In the light of forgiveness, Jesus said, "Let him who is without sin among you be the first to throw a stone at her, (John 8:7)." And therefore, to the new generation, parents who have renewed their minds refer to the new generation to always remember the above verse of the Scripture. It probably means that everyone in this world is fallible. That actually does not mean that you would not endeavor to make good selection, in order to prevent any pitfall. In effect, the contemporary life requires open relationship at every level in order to balance out the past and the present facts.

In transmitting the oral traditions, Congolese parents both father and mother would touch the issues of being resistant to strangers' influences in order to prevent being misled once again, by the phony missionaries and their collaborators, who deceived the King of Kongo, at the earlier time. He was eventually naïve and did not use his God's given wisdom or discernment to read between the lines.

In fact, it is human nature for youth to raise all types of questions concerning a situation that need more clarifications. As a matter of fact, while communicating with senior citizens, the new generation keeps on asking fiery questions repeatedly, "Was the King of Kongo, a weak- minded individual? Was he a naïve man? How could he possible not ensure the safety of his fellowman? Was he induced or blinded by the early missionaries' wrong appearance? Was he just a victim of circumstance?" He apparently did not sense any danger of dealing with mischief individuals; who had entered his Kingdom-in the name of God; since deceitfulness was unknown to the culture of his ancestors. Today, the youth react strongly to the King's weakness. The fiery students asked, "What would happen to King Nzinga-Nkuvu if he had been alive today?" Would the youth stone him to death, for his frailty which had gotten us in such entanglements?

Actually, as the children are growing up, intellectually, they are developing a desire to know all the necessary details regarding the past and present cultural as well social issues. And therefore, they prefer to receive that knowledge from the source, or from their family live historians, rather than relying on the written textbooks which may not be completely accurate. Probably this is due to misinterpretations and communication gaps. The Congolese mothers, however, signal their daughters to be one step ahead. In essence, a woman is caring, patient, compassionate, and she loves to protect everyone involved in the community. She was given a powerful insight.

And therefore, when dealing with strangers, mothers sound a warning to their daughters, "Beware and be alert!" Use your motherhood's insight to prevent male's frailty." In reality, female parents often refer to the error which the King of Kongo had unfortunately made, due to his weakness and hospitality. Mothers also remind their daughters, "Remember, the King's leadership had permitted the tragedy, which cannot be remedied, historically speaking. So, do not therefore, fail to remember that when a male Chief demonstrates weakness in terms of overseeing situations, according to the oral traditions, a female individual from the same family immediately, should take over the leadership, because a female individual has a keen sense of direction. And intuitively, she perceives things which might occur in the near future." This is what happened in the past; the oral traditions relate that, when the King failed to save the kingdom, the Queen had endeavored in saving the Kingdom afterwards *(Read, "Africa presents the Congo RDC and the Congolese Woman Chief)* by Bepona Collection."

REWARDING CHILDREN FOR THEIR ENDEAVORS

The majority of the Congolese parents believe that children should be rewarded for all the necessary efforts they have made in order to achieve their educations, and eventually have received a degree, diploma, or a certificate.

Below is an example of a student who had a longing desire to visit *LAKE TANGANYIKA* which she had studied in School. Ms. Manika Ngangoli had been rewarded travel accommodations by her beloved family who had been fortunately able to afford it. That special trip was merely to fulfill her yearning desire of visiting the famous Lake Tanganyika. She had said to herself, 'Studying about it in School was fine, but having a real experience of being there in my tangible and physical body would be just perfect." Ultimately, her longing desire to step on that particular spot was accomplished satisfactorily.

It is necessary to indicate however that not every parent is obligated to satisfy their children in the same manner. Children and their parents interact with each others, and therefore they know how to go about it. Parents are required to meet such needs based on their financial ability. Kids also do compromise with their parents; they would then settle with whatever their parents can actually effort at that time. Modest families for instance, organize a simple family gathering. With respect to simplicity, children are warned to refrain from being envious as that awful desire could bring miseries in their lives.

VISITING LAKE TANGANYIKA

(The second largest lake in Africa)

Manika Ngangoli's dream has come through, at last. She said, "I see you "My Famous Lake Tanganyika" in my tangible body. I am now able to touch your water and your sand with satisfaction!" Ms Manika Ngangoli is so grateful to her parents for allowing her to fulfill her dream of visiting the famous "LAKE TANGANYIKA," which she had studied and had taken several exams while she was in school in the capital city.

Why did Manika have such a yearning desire to visit Lake Tanganyika after her High School Graduation?

Manika replied, "Growing in the capital city far away from Southern East area, I was fascinated to learn about **Lake Tanganyika's magnitude and its variety of species.** In fact my Geography teacher had made the class very lively so I was excited to one day go and visit it this famous lake.

I truly held a vivid picture in my mind to be there one day, in my physical and tangible body; until I am able to touch the water and the sand of Lake Tanganyika. Further, I was being impressed to learn about the fishing activity, which goes on over that Lake. And therefore, I had planned to view it in person without fail. Probably, this desire may be undervalued by another individual, who does not perceive it as being excited to actually be there in person. However, because I value the history of my country dearly, and all of its resources, it was worthy for me to visit it. This was something I had really wanted to do; certainly nothing else in the world would have substituted this valuable gift. On one hand, I did not want to put any burden on my folks, but I knew somehow, that they had some possibilities to finance my trip for one week to this area, especially that I had a cousin stationed in Lubumbashi city.

Words fail me utterly to express myself how I had enjoyed viewing the spectacular of fishing boats which were lined up over Lake Tanganyika, and especially perceiving it at nights! What a beautiful scene to observe! It would appear as though Lake Tanganyika had actually become such a luminous huge city; brightened by all the lights coming from different directions of various fishing boats. The surface of the water would be lit by that white and golden lights shooting simultaneously from every direction, making the view exciting to look into. Further, one would view the crew from different boats, casting theirnets in the water; and pulling out slowly, and catching huge, and various exotic tasty fishes. At the end, the boats would be full of diverse fishes of various sizes. The boats will be returning back to the shoreline rapidly, and all of them would be lined up one after the other. Another thing, the workers of each boat would gather around their boat in order to start sorting out and placing fishes in their proper containers, which were being prepared to be exported to various parts of the world. Manika said, "I inquired the reason why they had to export African fish to various part of the world that have extensive fishing activities?" She was told, "Reportedly, those fishes are very healthy and tasty too, because they are grown from unpolluted water. And therefore, they are very expensive in those countries; such luxury is reserved exclusively for the wealthy people." Nevertheless, the whole thing was quite a spectacular to observe!" Manika reported eagerly.

Ultimately, I can conclude that, my longing desire to visit Lake Tanganyika would have never been fulfilled, if my parents had not had a high degree of love for me. They knew that I was a hard working daughter. Further, I maintained good school records. In addition, I was very active and participated in various school activities. Also, I was always selected to perform some important academic activities. Moreover, I graduated with honor. Those are the facts which please all the good parents, I think. Because of my endeavors, my parents were pleased with me. And they too, *wanted to make me happy, in order to prove how much they were proud of me, for having listened to their advice. And also, I had practiced what they had taught me in regard to our oral traditional law, so currently, I am aware of all the historical past and present events which make our contemporary history viable.*

Celebration of School Achievement

Congratulation to
Imiri and Mindaya
Registered Nurses

PARENTS *AND CHILDREN WORK HARMONIOUSLY IN ORDER TO ACHIEVE A SUCCESSFUL RESULT*.

Imiri and Mindala have worked hard and have successfully achieved their Nursing School. They have demonstrated their willingness to become self-sufficient as the culture requires it. Therefore, their parents are honored. They are extremely happy, and for that reason, all the family members and friends would gather together in order to celebrate for their graduation, as well as to congratulate them for honoring their respective families. Because the family rejoices extremely during such occasion, friends and families offer special gifts to the graduates.

Basically, Congolese parents organize a big dinner in the honor their child's graduation, which is regarded as a big family event. Generally, family and friends come together to partake in the celebration. Usually, after having dinner, family members and friends who wish to offer any gift will do so. The types of gift to offer is optional, some gifts are in terms of monetary, others come in any different nature. In fact, all depends on the individual's volition and on his or her financial capability.

During the graduation ceremony parents are overwhelmed with joy. Customarily, family expresses that exhilaration by shouting, "At last the seed which we had sowed has blossomed, and yielded us a positive result." Congolese parents ensure to advise their children in the following manner, "Remember, no matter what happens in your life, never neglect your child today, because you will never know, what the future has in store for that kid; especially, when you actually nurture it with love and perseverance." Parents' affection is a greater remedy for the development of a healthy and happy child.

Conclusion

As we have discussed throughout this book, in the Bantu/Congolese culture, the course of "Child Education" is designed in such a natural way. It is empirical, so to speak, or the knowledge is based solely from experience, particularly from sensory observations. It does not require any predetermined concepts or pre-established rules.

The method of educating a child does not require any sophisticated or complicated steps. It does not entail any social science terminologies either. The African style of educating a child is moderately simple. Parents are naturally gifted. They apply the process of perception; and we can therefore conclude that parents have actually developed a power of observation. In reality, the ability of nurturing a child appropriately has been originated from our ancestors' virtues inspired by our Nzambe/Nzambi-Mpungu/Mungu, the Great Being from Heaven who requires perpetual justice and harmony. And from this understanding, the Bantu peoples believe that in order to obtain a good result in rearing a child, rules and regulations should be established around the family, and they should be re-inforced systematically.

In essence, African parents are known to have an exceptional discipline when raising their children as we have illustrated in this book. However, Critics from different societies view this procedure as being extremely strict in regard to disciplining their offspring in terms of learning the proper behaviors, around the family, as well as in public. Nevertheless, to African culture, it is regarded as being essential. This does not imply that the child is being nurtured austerely. In despite of that appearance, parents take the disciplinary steps with a lot of love and compassion.

Congolese parents underline the old saying, "It is better to shape the tree while it is still tiny than wait until it grows, and gets out of shape." They deem that when a good seed has been planted on a good soil, eventually it has to blossom and yield good fruits. Parents believe that giving birth is one thing, but rearing that child in the society that is filled with injustice and treachery is another thing altogether. Further, it is quite a process to follow; surely, it requires a combination of love, compassion and also a disciplinary action, including punishments.

Therefore, good parents cannot be afraid of reprimanding a child who is misbehaving around the family, or in public area, just because of its age. This can be referred to the Bantu/Congolese expression which states, ***"When you are toasting peanuts, you should not stop the process, just because you are embarrassed to follow that activity."*** What would happen if you do? All those peanuts would get eventually burned. That certainly, would not be wise. Thus, parents should know that a child's error should be nipped in the bud since its early days in order to prevent its re-occurrence. Therefore, an intelligent parent should not be embarrassed in reprimanding a child who is going astray.

In effect, most of the Congolese parents have developed a special sign of reprimanding a child who is acting mischievously in public. When a child behaves badly in public, a mother could just glance at that kid, without voicing a word. And then, in the twinkling of an eye, that child would immediately recall that its mother actually disapproves of his or her behavior. Evidently, as a result of being troublesome or for embarrassing its folks, that child would have to undergo a serious punishment, once it arrives at its parents' home. Such is a discretionary manner of correcting a child's behavior in public, as far as the Congolese parents are concerned, in that manner. In addition, the Congolese parents judge that it is necessary, sometimes for a parent to act sternly or firmly with certain kids in order to correct their stubbornness or disobedience.

However, parents do not quite act rigorously, or harshly as the critics presume. Certain individuals keep on believing that African parents are rude with their children. However, African parents argue that, because they are aware of the society's disease of duplicity, which has been going on for decades in this world, so, folks take the responsibility of alerting the younger generation that, the society as a whole, exhibits a high degree of injustice almost in every level, and therefore, in order to cope with the world of disloyalty, a child should be given a little push in order to strengthen it, mentally, morally, physically, and spiritually; so it does not get fooled easily (referring to **King Nzinga-Nkuvu's mistakes of the 15th century**.) which had permitted the concealment of the true historical facts, through diplomatic and religious relationship scheme.

Regarding spiritual or religious education, as we have previously mentioned, religious families take the responsibility of *gradually revealing spiritual truth* to their children. Parents also disclose the reason why a kid should be anchored in the belief of Nzambe/Mungu/or Nzambi-Mpungu, the Great Being, opposed to those children who are raised in the pagan environments. The Congolese children whom parents are still alive are privileged indeed to receive deep spiritual understanding, opposed to destitute or orphans kids who had completely lost their immediate or even extended families through the incessant war.

Those kids are unfortunately growing without any type of spiritual, intellectual, cultural or traditional knowledge, due to the selfishness, as well as to the poor leadership in the land. Because these children lack proper guidance, there is no one to shape them appropriately. As a result, they would not build any solid foundation in regard to their future society, because they would have no firm beliefs concerning their traditions, consequently, those children would not know how to behave in a way that is morally good or acceptable with their associations. Ultimately, they would fail to apply the principles of justice, fairness and honesty.

And therefore, instead of contributing constructively, their contribution would be negative in the society and in the world. Would these children be to blame for their ignorance? Why should they? These children would have nothing to remember from their childhood. They would not be able to state that, "When I was young, my parents/my grandparents/my great grandparents had told me that such and such thing was morally, socially or culturally unacceptable.

Because the youth is only a victim of the social dilemma, the leaders therefore, should take the responsibility of remedying such situations, especially in the country where there is no scarcity of resources such as the Congo RDC. There is apparently, no reason why children should be neglected or prevented from acquiring all the benefits which they are entitled to. Obviously the increase in the number of illiteracy in their land would entail the increase in the level of poverty. As a result, this group of children would not be enlightened enough in recovering their heritage and restore their human dignity, if nobody reaches out to help them today. They would once again be driven in the pit where their ancestors' traditions would be once again stigmatized.

Certainly, kids who come from aggressive or pagan families usually are the ones who express antagonism against the latest missionaries, because they strongly argue that "Whether it is the early or the latest missionaries, all of them should be put in the same boat; because they actually have the same negative motive when it comes to dealing with the people of our land." These individuals have built their fierce beliefs in this area. They argue always referring to the fact that they had noticed no positive changes throughout the land in spite of those individuals' presence there. And yet, these religious organizations have been coming in their land since 15th century.

People actually perceive no signs or wonders. They see no spiritual manifestations, so why should they believe in missionaries' scenarios? Apparently, there is a spiritual battle that has been going on between both areas, or between both of these views, as we have indicated earlier. Therefore, any evangelization activities pertaining to those individuals should really be reserved only to the true anointed servants of God, who could exemplify the power of the Living God as their practice requires it in order to win the lost souls in this particular world.

Furthermore, parents replied to critics that regardless of the appearance, they correct their children without any slightest idea of harming them. That belief was inherited from their ancestors. And therefore, it is embedded in their minds. The disciplinary measures are just the way to bring the awareness of family's requirements to the infant. The new generation had adopted it, as being the appropriate means of rearing a child in order to obtain a positive result.

Moreover, African parents feel that they must ensure a proper guidance in the attempt to prevent any future pitfall or deviation. In order to exemplify their concern about their children, African women prefer to drag their children, if necessary, to wherever they could possibly go with them. This actually is one of the reasons why an African mother has always been portrayed, carrying her child on her back. In reality, she does it for security measures. Further, this signifies that that woman does not trust her neighbors or her acquaintances enough in order to request any type of baby sitting assistance from them. And therefore, she prefers to have her child tied on her back in order to ensure its security. However, the disciplinary action must be taken in order to better nurture that child. In fact, regardless of how high the degree of her love might be for her child, a Congolese mother takes an appropriate discipline of educating her kid. She says, "If I desire my child to learn appropriately and be rooted, or anchored in its traditions or heritage, it has to be right now or never.

In spite of all the criticism which African parents undergo, Congolese parents and their children agree with such disciplinary actions, because it prevents the child to experience the negative outcome in the future, and the kid shall always recall, what Mama had told her since her childhood. Therefore, the African culture deems that prevention is better than cure. Most of the people in the Congolese society had actually confirmed that good parents are those who are not afraid to reprimand or punish belligerent kids with love and compassion, of course.

Furthermore, Congolese parents think that children must also be instructed to start taking certain initiatives around the house. It has to be a cooperative action in the family circle. Everyone ought to contribute to the best of his or her ability. Each person should fill in a daily task. The tasks required would vary from family to family. It also depends on the locality where the families have been settled down. Additionally, parents make it clear to their children that, they should not be in a position of begging, or borrowing from anyone. They should rather be the producers, or the providers, or the lenders and not the other way around. Because God has already provided everything, which will make an individual self-sufficient (everyone was given a brain and muscles), so there is no apparent reason, why anyone would choose to be a burden to another family member. Therefore, in order to gain respect in the society, every person should begin contributing constructively in the household activities as well as in the society.

Currently,, Congolese parents are concerned about their children's school education; although the educational system has been affected by the incessant war which the country has been a victim for several decades now, nevertheless, kids are encouraged in the following manners: "Child, you make sure to go to school, and study well until the completion of your education.

Subsequently, you will have to work and earn your living honestly." Congolese parents also highlight the following statement, *"CHILD DO NOT BE A LETHARGIC PERSON IN LIFE,"* and also avoid any association with individuals that may get you involved in swindling activities. Know that those individuals dishonor their families as well as their God, by **STEALING or getting enmeshed in the wrong activities!"** Parents also sound a warning such as, "Never take anything which does not belong to you by all means. – *Our ancestors had called such action, "Koyiba" (koh-yee-bah) or (Stealing - THAT*

MEANS, ACQUIRING SOMEONE ELSE'S BELONGINGS WITHOUT HAVING ANY AUTHORIZATION TO DO SO. Please remember always, ***"SHOULD YOU FIND ANYTHING ON YOUR WAY, WHETHER MONEY, A PIECE OF CLOTTHING, SHOES, BAG, OR ANYTHING WHATSOEVER WHICH YOU HAVE NOT EARNED THE RIGHT TO HAVE IT**, by all means, leave that item where you have found it; so that whoever who had dropped it there, by accident would walk back that way and find it there.* **Remember do not pick it up!"** Folks also would add, "Such practice is what our ancestors had called integrity which the new generation is required to practice. We were told to follow after their footsteps so our oral traditions would be maintained flawlessly. Also, bear in mind that a society necessitates peace, love, integrity, loyalty, harmony, justice, and especially respect, if it needs to be sustained."

Ultimately, The Bantu/Congolese society highlights the historical facts which had led the land into a pitfall – association with unkind people had brought things which our ancestors had rejected and which are considered to be a TABOO in our history. As a matter of fact, the action of *STEALING or CONFISCATING ANY ITEM WHICH YOU DID NOT EARN, FROM THAT OWNER, SUCH THING IS UNACCEPTABLE, INDEED. That is Disgrace, because* that action really STINKS, as far as our ancestors 'belief is concerned. SO, PLEASE, REFRAIN FROM TAKING

SUCH ACTION. It brings a severe natural punishment in life from which nobody can extricate himself or herself no matter what that individual does. In effect, that punishment is also known as a **Curse**!

Evidently, some critics argue that African people are superstitious, because they are always talking and warning their children about the word "**Curse.**" However, African parents respond that the word curse exists way before we were all born. This word appears practically in many different languages; in English for instant it is known as a, "Curse," in French it is referred to, as la "**Malediction,**" in Congolese languages such as in Kikongo it is called, **Kolakidila** (Ko lah-kee-dee-lah) in Lingala language it is referred to as "**Kolakila (ko-lah-kee-lah)**," and in Spanish this word is known as , **la "Maledicion."** Therefore, the word curse was not originated from African ancestors, but it has been here since the creation of this universe. It is found in the Holy Scripture (Bible), and therefore, no individual can actually escape the consequences of his or her own mistakes. In regard to this topic, the wise people had actually warned us repeatedly that "Whatever a man does in his life, will always come back to him or her, one way or the other, and soon or later, be it good or bad." *Children are advised to know the following statement, "Remember that the law of cause and effect does not discriminate*." This is in fact the reason why the Congolese parents while educating their children feel the necessity of underlining all the details pertaining to this particular topic. They go deep into it. They know how to elaborate it, and make it vivid. In fact, parents relate various examples, which capture the child' mind. Because this knowledge is estimated to be crucial; the culture requires parents to lay emphasis on the young generation's mind; so that they too, would orally pass it to the new generation to come. Thus, they shall be free, and remain self-sufficient instead of becoming thieves, beggars, or be dependent upon anyone else in the family or in the society, and especially upon those in the world, who would tend to impoverish others by taking away whatever really belongs to the children pretending to offer them a tiny portion of their own wealth, which would undervalue them eventually.

Ultimately, by revealing some historical facts to the children, or to the younger generation, we are not inferring that the youth should develop hostility, retaliation, or resentment in dealing with various people of different backgrounds. Further, we do not intend to instill any negativity in the youth's minds either. Our main motive is to reveal and expose reality of our historical facts past and present which would help the younger generation to broaden their knowledge as they precede their journey in this world of injustice, and full of intrigues.

Our goal is to be able to urge the youth to be anchored in the knowledge of their ancestors' virtues, which would reflect their personal identities, and live ethically. Also to advising it to endeavor in maintaining and sustaining the reality of their backgrounds, so that these qualities may be flawlessly transmitted to the future generation. In essence, children are required to remember their basic family education such as hygiene, and keep up with a refinement appearance. Kids ought to bear in mind the necessity of practicing the word sharing, as opposed to selfishness; having compassion, instead of being indifferent to the suffering of others; and also, acting with integrity, loyalty, as well as showing respect to everyone without rationalizing any evil activity.

Finally, parents insist on the following statement: "Children, be vigilant in whatever you shall do in life; and just remember, our ***NZAMBE/NZAMBI-MPUNGU/MUNGU*** (the *Great Being in Heaven*) loves everyone of Its creature. And therefore, try to be alert, especially; learn to distinguish between the words justice and injustice, because there is no middle ground, thus be not a part of injustice, either in the support of it, or in its acceptance. At last, remember our key word which has been referred to us as,"BOTOSI (boh-toh-se/LUZITU (lo-u-ze-to-u), which means RESPECT."

FINISH

Word of appreciation to our Readers

To all our readers, we wish to thank you for taking the time to read this book written in such a simple language, terms and styles. The resources found in this book are real or factual. All the photographs came from the Congo RDC, Central Africa, which is the Bantu/Congolese society. The pictures illustrate children daily 'activities, as well as their experiences around the families, homes and schools. We have attempted to cover almost all the areas, urban as well as rural activities.

In essence, our inference would be as follow: "Child Education," as we have humbly discussed in this book may vary slightly from family to family, and from area to area, because it does not require any predefined rules, as was previously indicated. Further, it could also vary from society to society; nevertheless, any good parents would look forward to seeing the success of their endeavors in rearing that child. The end product of all their efforts is what really matters.

When a child turns out to be constructive in the society, and demonstrates all the good qualities required, this would denote that that kid has honored its parents, as well as its ancestors. That child would be an asset in building the foundation of the society. That individual would be able to maintain and sustaining the norms required in protecting its true identity from being stigmatized. In fact, the topic of Child Education in the Bantu/Congolese society is not limited to school education alone, but it encompasses traditional education as well.

ACKNOWLEDGEMENT

We recognize the fact that there is no individual who can claim to know everything on this earth, besides from God. Therefore, we offer our first gratitude to God who had inspired us in bringing forth this work.

Further, we are compelled to acknowledge everyone who had assisted us in the outer world such as our family members, friends and educators. Everyone of them had contributed extensively in helping us to accomplish this work.

We also would like to extend our sincere thanks to all the kids that are found in this book, as well as to their teachers who had been very cooperative in participating in our research, as well as allowing us to take their photographs which are illustrated in this book.

BEPONA BOOKS

Africa Presents

- The Congo RDC and Lingala Language (English and French version (First edition) - **LINGALA DICTIONARY /ENGLISH/FRENCH.**

- The Congo RDC and Kikongo Language (English and French version (first edition). **KIKONGO DICTIONARY /ENGLSIH/FRENCH**

- The Congo RDC and Child Education (First edition)

- The Congo RDC and Congolese Cuisine (First edition)

- The Congo RDC and A Congolese Woman Chief (Mfumu-Mkento)

- Le Congo RDC Et la Femme Dirigeante (Mfumu-Nkento)

- The Congo RDC and Congolese Tradition Law (first edition)

- The Congo RDC and Congolese Comedy/Novels

    1. A Mysterious Boy called Timo Mikwaya Well known as Kamina (novel)

    2. Mr. Aleyi-Atondi

       How can this man live with his In-laws for over 15 years? (Novel)

    3. A Western Professor with an African University Student (Abelengezi) - novel

    4. Experience of two African young ladies in America (Magoke) - novel

    By

Bepona Collection

Books' Samples

Africa presents the Congo RDC and A Congolese Woman chief (Mfumu-Nkento (**pronounced uhm-foomoo-kan-too**)

English   Français

Africa presents the Congo RDC and **Child Education in the Bantu society**

Africa presents the Congo RDC and **Congolese Cuisine**

Africa presents the Congo RDC and Lingala Language English French versions

Africa presents the Congo RDC and Kikongo ya l'Etat English and French versions

Africa presents the Congo RDC and **Tradinal law (Common law)**

ABOUT BEPONA COLLECTION

The authors of "Bepona Books" are female Congolese-American. We write about the culture of the Bantu society of the Congo RDC, which is located in Central Africa (MPA, PAS, BBA, and BA).

Our books are apolitical. They are based on our personal research conducted scholarly and confirmed by oral traditions of the Bantu peoples, transmitted to us by our live Historians. In fact, the live historians are the wise living senior citizens who continue to maintain and sustain the authenticity of the traditions flawlessly or without any distortion.

Our readers will notice that the titles of all our books in English are prefaced with, "Africa Presents the Congo RDC," and then, are followed by the actual book titles. The titles of all our books in French are prefaced with, "L' Afrique Présente Le Congo RDC," and then, followed by the actual book titles. Actually, we purposely took this approach, because we realize that not everyone is proficient in Geography. Apparently, certain individuals still believe that Africa is a country rather than a Continent. It is therefore, necessary to clarify the fact that the Congo RDC is a country within this particular Continent and not the other way around.

In writing about the Bantu/Congolese culture, we have preferred to focus on the most important social topics, namely, "Traditional law (Common law), Congolese woman's leadership, Congolese cuisine, Child education, and two major Congolese languages (called Lingala, Kikongo ya l'Etat and their related dictionaries) - Concerning our novels, they are based on the daily cultural events. The original characters and settings are withheld intentionally in order to protect the privacy of those concerned.

All our books are written in simple terms, language and style. Our goal is to humbly share our culture with individuals, who are interested in diversity, and also, to express ourselves, but not to impress our readers. Ultimately, in regard to the bibliography, we owe all our credits to the Bantu live historians from the Congo RDC who have been willing to disclose their knowledge to us.

I-Picture depicts: Assembly of diverse High School Students at ATHENEE SQUARE, in Kinshasa City, Congo, RDC – 1969

I -Picture

II – Picture *Illustrates Elementary Students in the rural area in the Congo RDC*

Here children are all scattered during their class break.

KINSHASA, THE CAPITAL CITY OF THE DEMOCRATIC REPUBLIC OF CONGO, PRIOR TO THE CIVIL WAR

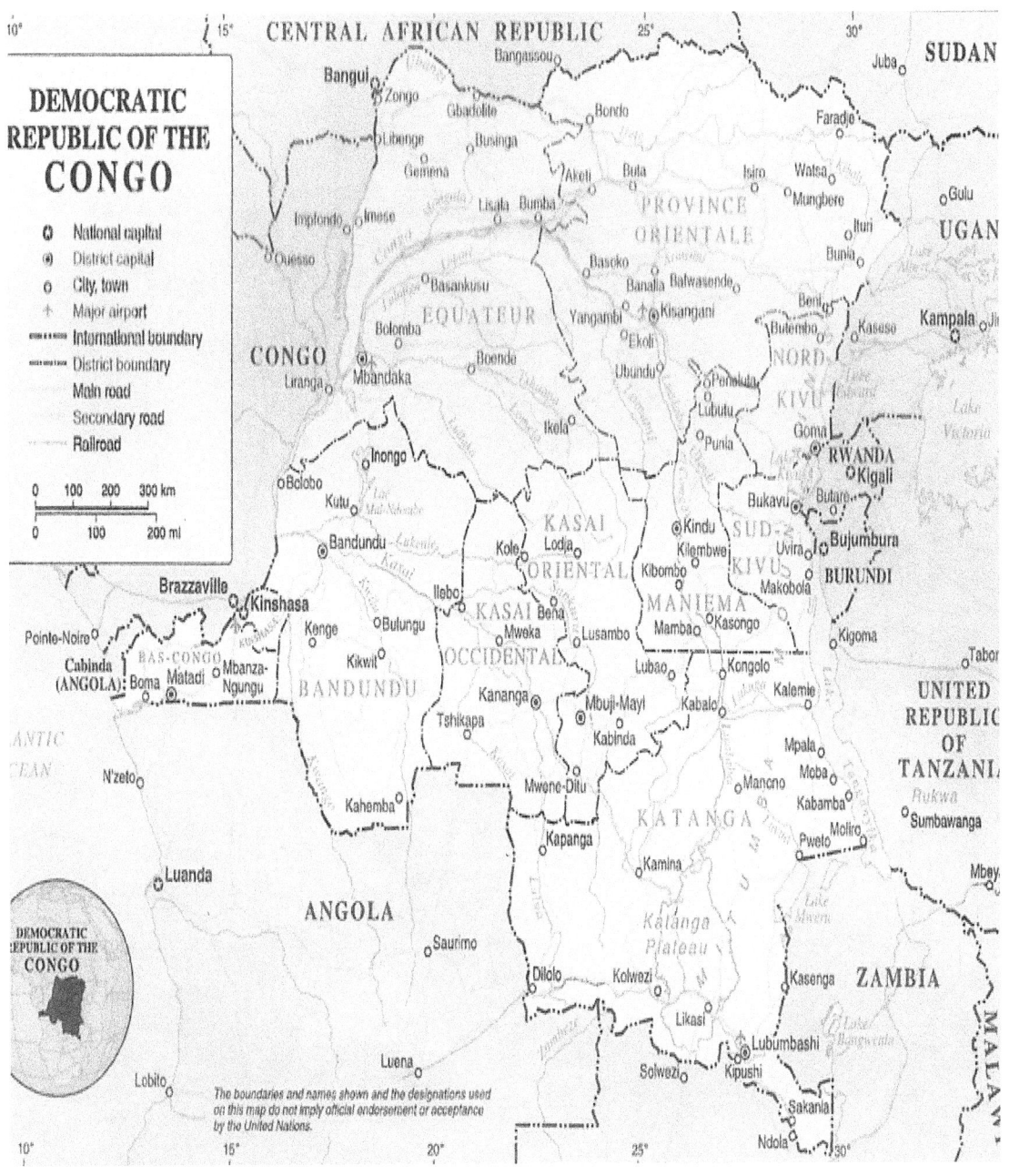

AFRICA

INDEX

A

About Bepona Collection , page 112

Acknowledgment, page 109

Addressing people, ch. II, page 41,

B

Bepona Books, page 112

Books' samples, page 111

C

Celebrating School Achievement, ch. IV, page 94

Child's responsibilities, ch.I, page 31

Child Care from infant to childhood, ch. I, page 37

Child Safety, ch. page 53

Children behaviors at Home & In the Society, ch. I, page 51

Conclusion, page 95

Congolese Father's View, ch. I, page 36

Contrasting Urban vs Rural Areas Students , ch.III, page 56

Cultural Education, ch. III, page 72

D

Dedication, page 8

Daily Routine, ch.I, page 29

D

Developing Child Safety Measures, ch. I, page 35

H

Highlighting appropriate Manners, ch. 2 page.49

O

Overview, page 9

R

Relationship between Congolese Parents and Their Children, ch. III, page 62

Rewarding Children for Their Endeavors, ch.. IV, page 90

Rules and Regulations, ch. II, page 38

U

Urban Children, ch. I, page.34

W

Word of appreciation to our readers, page 108

www.ingramcontent.com/pod-product-compliance
Lightning Source LLC
Chambersburg PA
CBHW080553230426
43663CB00015B/2820